TADWEEN PUBLIS

Tadween Publishing, a new form of "publishing house," is part of the *A*... institute that has run four organizations since 1992: the peer-reviewed publication, *Arab Studies Journal*, the electronic publication, *Jadaliyya*, the research institute, *FAMA* (Forum on Arab and Muslim Affairs), and the documentary collective, *Quilting Point*.

Middle East Studies Pedagogy Initiative (MESPI)

In cooperation with the Middle East Studies Program at George Mason University, Tadween is launching the Middle East Studies Pedagogy Initiative (MESPI) to provide critical, user-friendly, and informative pedagogical material and instruction to educators in the field and beyond. MESPI will build on two counts: Educators Networks and Pedagogical Resources. Tadween's Educators Network (TEN) provides members with complementary copies of Tadween Publications intended for the classroom. If you are an educator, please sign up to TEN here to receive your complimentary copies. MESPI will be producing Pedagogical Publications intended primarily for the classroom, covering various countries, topics, events, themes, and paradigms. Starting with our pilot project, JADMAG, these publications will be produced on a regular basis and will be accompanied by resources for further examination of the subject matter.

www.TADWEENPUBLISHING.com

Gaza in Context

Caption: Still from *Gaza in Context*

Contents

JADMAG

Development as a Mechanism of Control

Gendered Violence of Settler Colonialism

About the Authors

Pedagogical and Media Resources

More from Tadween

Still from *Gaza in Context*

Noura Erakat and Tareq Radi

In the summer 2014, Israel launched its most devastating offensive on the besieged Gaza Strip to date. It sealed the perimeters, expanded the buffer zones, concentrated the already dense population, and launched six thousand airstrikes and fifty thousand artillery shells in an air and ground offensive that lasted for fifty-one days. The register of death and destruction was harrowing and included the killing of 2,251 Palestinians, including 551 children; the complete or severe destruction of eighteen thousand homes; the forcible displacement of one hundred thousand Palestinians, and untold trauma that has left more than three-hundred thousand children in need of psycho-social treatment. Palestinian forces killed seventy-two Israelis, six of whom were civilians. As Palestinian doctors struggled to treat the injured in under resourced hospitals vulnerable to attack, Israel's military industry boomed. Three hundred employees of one company, Israel Military Industries, worked twenty-four hour shifts for four weeks, to ensure that the Israeli Army would have a sufficient arsenal. One company CEO explained, "After every campaign of the kind that is now taking place in Gaza, we see an increase in the number of customers from abroad..." because they can market their weapons as "battle-tested." Indeed, Gaza's captive population has become a laboratory for means and methods of warfare.

Despite overwhelming evidence of the disparity of power between Israel and all Palestinians, as well as the aggressiveness of Israel's exercise of its power including excessive and brutal violence and collective punishment in Gaza in the form of occupation, siege, and frequent military assaults against dense and captive civilian populations, mainstream media and educational materials continue to frame Israel as the victim. The harshest critique of Israel's unparalleled use of force during its Summer 2014 offensive was that it was "too much," implicitly suggesting that the colonial relationship between Israel and its captive subjects is normal. Instead, pundits, analysts, and journalists reserved the realm of abnormality for Palestinians who used crude weapons to challenge their condition. By emphasizing the

role of Hamas and diminishing the question of Palestine, Israel has collapsed conditions in Gaza with asymmetric conflicts, or what has come to be known as the "global war on terror," thus eliding the consequential distinctions between Palestinians and other non-state actors. Together, the practice of systematic war and the framework of unique distinction have set the Gaza Strip apart from the question of Palestine. This compendium uses Operation Protection Edge (OPE) to demonstrate the temporal and spatial continuity of Israel's settler-colonial policies across Israel and the Occupied Territories in order to disrupt the language of exceptionalism surrounding the Gaza Strip today. It scrutinizes Israeli settler-colonialism through a multi-disciplinary lens including history, law, development, political economy, and gender.

While the scope of force deployed during OPE is unprecedented, Israeli warfare is not. The summer 2014 offensive was the eighth attack on the coastal enclave since unilateral disengagement in 2005 and the twenty-second attack since the exchange of letters between Prime Minister Ariel Sharon and President George W. Bush in April 2004. In her contribution, originally published in The Nation, Noura Erakat surveys Israel's aggressions towards Gaza and concludes that warfare is systemic, systematic and longstanding, and is an extension of Israel's broader policy towards all Palestinians. This policy is guided by two principles: to obtain the maximum amount of Palestinian land with the minimum number of Palestinian people and to concentrate a maximum number of Palestinians onto a minimum amount of land. Through this analysis, Erakat rehabilitates the question of the Gaza Strip within a framework of settler-colonialism that helps put the rest of the pieces within this pedagogical publication in conversation with one other.

Joel Beinin scrutinizes examples of incitement made by Israel's governing officials that exemplify the "public devaluation of Arab life." He does so to expose the normalization of anti-Arab and anti-Muslim sentiments in Israeli society. For example, Uri Elitzur, a pro-settlement journalist and former aide to Prime Minister Benyamin Netanyahu, argued that all Palestinians are enemy combatants and that rape should be used as a tool to deter Palestinian resistance. Beinin argues that this racism lays the foundation for domestic support of military operations and serves to shield the army from critiques of disproportionate uses of force.

While Beinin scrutinizes the societal trends that have shielded Israel's army from domestic accountability, Erakat's article on Israel's manipulation of the laws of war helps explain how such expanded force is legitimated in the language of law. She explains that Israel's unprecedented use of force during OPE is a reflection of the new norms of war it has sought to establish since the second intifada in September 2000. She unpacks some of Israel's most troubling claims including a radical understanding of force-protection, a forward-looking analysis of proportionality, and a truncated definition of who is a Palestinian civilian. Erakat concludes that as a result of these changes in the law together with Israel's long-standing policy towards Palestinians, OPE may not be the worst of what is to come.

> *Despite the imbalance of military force, as well as the structural violence of siege, media narratives of victimhood and survival were exclusively reserved for Israel and Israelis.*

The four articles on development critically examine how states and international organizations deliberately and/or inadvertently use development policy to further subjugate, separate, and weaken Palestinian society. As Gaza's economy reaches the highest stages of de-development yet, Sara Roy, Nuriya Oswald, and Max Ajl each scrutinize the international community's futile policies adopted to "reconstruct" Gaza in the aftermath of OPE's devastation.

Roy reaffirms that Israel's attack on Gaza was not a response to Hamas rocket fire, but rather, continued its policy of incapacitating the coastal enclave. Roy highlights that not a single reconstruction plan has challenged the political status quo that produces the Gaza Strip's vulnerability and deprivation. She argues that the current plans further entrench Israel's blockade and outsource the responsibility for its maintenance to the United Nations thus legitimizing Israel's security narrative. Similarly, Oswald dissects the United Nation's Gaza Reconstruction Mechanism (GRM) to expose the economic benefits Israel may enjoy from the plan. She also tackles Israel's stated security concern regarding the application of imported materials towards military related activities. She highlights that, due to the current conditions in Gaza, recipients of the materials are unable to cover the cost of labor required for construction and, as a result, proceed to sell the items on the black market. Oswald argues that the absence of a mechanism to track how the materials are used once delivered reveals that the function of Israel's oversight is control rather than security.

Taking a step back, Ajl provides a historical analysis of the increasing scale of attacks on Gaza since 2006. He uses this historical analysis to interrogate the notion of "collapse" and its ability to separate Israeli policies from a settler-colonial frame-

work. Through a critical reading of the World Bank report Gaza Economy on the Verge of Collapse, Ajl argues that the "World Bank's analysis sidesteps the colonial genealogy of the siege" by attributing Israel's policies of warfare and blockade to the state's inability to reconcile with Hamas. In doing so, it elides the state's deliberate attempts to de-develop, isolate, and control the Gaza Strip since 1993, well before Hamas's electoral victory in 2006. The World Bank's economic prescriptions reflect this limited analysis. It recommends that lifting the siege and reforming the economy requires that the Palestinian Authority (PA) replaces Hamas as the governing body of Gaza. Ajl highlights that the World Bank's recommendation to work with the PA is colonial in nature, because it only accepts and supports interlocutors that the colonial power has deemed legitimate.

As Roy and Oswald point out, the GRM strengthens Israel's mechanisms of control over Gaza by granting Israel the authority to regulate the material that can enter the territory, but relieves it of any responsibility for the territory. Israel possesses a similar mechanism of control under the veneer of development in the West Bank. In her article, Lamya Hussain discusses the implications of the Israeli Civil Administration's (ICA) 2008 decision to appoint itself as the governing body that authorizes or denies any plans submitted by or on behalf of Palestinians in Area C. Today, the ICA serves as a planning regime designed to obstruct Palestinian development initiatives in order to take their spatial place. Hussain details the ICA's use of urban planning as a tool to facilitate housing demolitions, restrict mobility, annex resources, and shift local geographies.

Nur Arafeh's examination of Israeli policies aimed at removing Palestinians from Jerusalem rebuts the explanatory framework of religious conflict. She argues that Palestinian resistance in the city should be viewed as a response to colonial policies, as opposed to religious differences, and that religion is being exploited to obfuscate Israeli political goals. Furthermore, Arafeh criticizes the Palestinian Authority's lack of investment in Jerusalem as a contributing factor to the Judaization of the city. As Israeli development initiatives advance, leaderless Palestinians in Jerusalem are left to fend for themselves in the face of forced displacement and economic strangulation.

The formal leadership's apathy towards Jerusalem is part of a broader context of Palestinian cooptation and inefficacy. In his contribution on security coordination with Israel, Tariq Dana identifies the major factors that transformed the Palestinian security sector into a proxy apparatus of Israel's occupation regime. Upon Hamas's legislative victory in 2007, Israel and its Western allies moved swiftly to support the PA in the West Bank and re-work the doctrinal foundation of Palestinian security. Over the next three years and with President Mahmoud Abbas's cooperation, the US State Department allocated ninety-nine million dollars to restructure the PA's security infrastructure and an additional 392 million dollars to train and equip its security forces. Together with other critical junctures, today the raison d'etre of Palestinian police forces is their ability to meet Israel's security concerns.

Mouin Rabbani uses the PA's fidelity to Israeli and American plans to scrutinize the potential of an impending intifada. He explains that the interlocking nature of the Palestinian security forces and the Israeli occupation, together with the Palestinian leadership's aversion to popular mobilization, makes resistance to Israel's colonial authority highly improbable. Despite the increasing ferocity of Israel's attacks, Rabbani notes that a third Palestinian mass uprising is unlikely because "rebellions are almost never instigated by reality alone." He highlights that the first and second intifadas were not simply reactions to particular events, rather they emerged and continued as a result of a confluence of cumulative factors that spanned several years. Rabbani sheds light on why and how a colonized people can endure sustained structural violence and not respond with sustained collective resistance.

Nadera Shalhoub-Kevorkian, Sarah Ihmoud and Suhad Dahir-Nashif center sexual violence as a tool within the larger structure of colonial domination. The authors draw on Patrick Wolfe's "logic of elimination," the understanding that settler colonialism is a structure and not a singular event that seeks to destroy and replace indigenous populations, to unpack Israel's racialized logic of sexual violence. Within this framework, genocide is intricately connected to settler colonialism. They expand on the sexualized discourses of OPE to demonstrate the embedded nature of sexual violence within Israel's eliminatory logic. Maya Mikdashi builds on this intersectional analysis of gender and settler colonialism by calling into question the lack of public mourning for Palestinian men killed during the large scale offensive. She takes a critical look at western-based media attention on the killing of women and children and argues it "further normalizes and erases the structures and successes of Israeli settler colonialism." Mikdashi asserts that the Palestinian people are one, regardless of their gender. They live together under settler colonial conditions and should not be separated in death, especially as even the most advanced weapons technology cannot distinguish them upon lethal contact.

The following contributions, combined with the previously published Gaza Revisited are a part of a larger pedagogical project titled, Gaza in Context. The centerpiece of the project is a 20-minute multimedia narrative documentary that combines lecture, animation, typography, and footage. In addition to the JadMags, the other components of the project include teaching guide for instructional purposes and a bibliography for research purposes. The project serves to rehabilitate the Gaza Strip within a settler-colonial framework. In doing so, the project emphasizes the non-exceptional nature of violence endured by Palestinians in the Gaza Strip. The articles in both volumes provide in-depth and multi-disciplinary resources that disrupt the current production of knowledge surrounding the "conflict." Operation Protective Edge, and any past or future Israeli onslaughts,

should be read within this framework in order to highlight the abnormality of the Palestinian condition and to realize a viable and just alternative.

Additional Gaza in Context Resources

- Pedagogical Module
- Research Resources
- Social Media Resources
- Blogs/Organizations
- Documentary Film

Available at www.gazaincontext.com

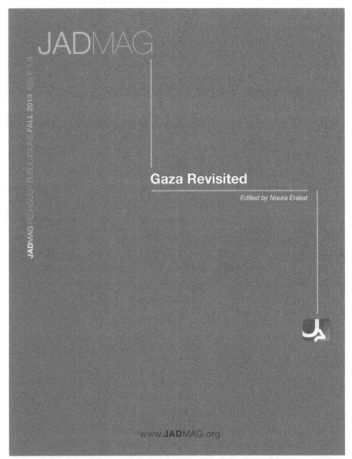

This pedagogy publication examines the November 2012 military offensive and unpacks historical legacies, legal questions, media portrayals, and political considerations. In doing so, the publication helps create a context for the attack and considers possibilities for the future of the conflict and the balance of power in the Middle East more generally. To purchase, visit www.tadweenpublishing.com.

Racism is the Foundation of Israel's Operation Protective Edge

Joel Beinin On 30 June Ayelet Shaked, chairwoman of the Knesset faction of the ultra-right wing ha-Bayit ha-Yehudi (Jewish Home) Party, a key member of the coalition government led by Prime Minister Netanyahu, posted on her Facebook page a previously unpublished article written by the late Uri Elitzur. Elitzur, a pro-settler journalist and former chief-of-staff to Netanyahu, wrote:

> Behind every terrorist stand dozens of men and women, without whom he could not engage in terrorism…They are all enemy combatants, and their blood shall be on all their heads. Now, this also includes the mothers of the martyrs, who send them to hell with flowers and kisses. They must follow their sons. Nothing would be more just. They should go, as well as the physical homes in which they raised the snakes. Otherwise, more little snakes will be raised there.

Shaked's post appeared the day the bodies of three abducted settler teens—Naftali Fraenkel, Gilad Shaar, and Eyal Yifrach—were discovered. It has since received more than 5,200 "likes."

For more than two weeks, Netanyahu and the media whipped the country into a hysterical state, accusing Hamas of responsibility for abducting the teens without providing evidence to support the claim and promoting hopes that they would be found alive, although the government knew that the boys were likely murdered within minutes of their abduction. Their deaths provided a pretext for more violent expressions of Israeli anti-Arab racism than ever before.

The viciousness of Mordechai Kedar, lecturer in Arabic literature at Bar Ilan University, was even more creative than Shaked and Elitzur's merely genocidal proposal. "The only thing that can deter terrorists like those who kidnapped the children and killed them," he said, "is the knowledge that their sister or their mother will be raped." As a university-based "expert," Kedar's heinous suggestion is based on his "understanding" of Arab culture. "It sounds very bad, but that is the Middle East," he explained, hastening to add, "I am not talking about what we should or should not do. I am talking about the facts."

Racism has become a legitimate, indeed an integral, component of Israeli public culture, making assertions like these seem "normal." The public devaluation of Arab life enables a society that sees itself as "enlightened" and "democratic" to repeatedly send its army to slaughter the largely defenseless population of the Gaza Strip—1.8 million people, mostly descendants of refugees who arrived during the 1948 Arab-Israeli war, and have been, to a greater or lesser extent, imprisoned since 1994.

Conciliatory gestures, on the other hand, are scorned. Just two days after Shaked's Facebook post, Orthodox Jews kidnapped sixteen-year-old Muhammad Abu Khdeir from the Shu'afat neighborhood of East Jerusalem and burned him alive in the Jerusalem Forest. Amir Peretz (Hatnua) was the only government minister to visit the grieving family. For this effort he received dozens of posts on his Facebook page threatening to kill him and his family. Meanwhile, vandals twice destroyed memorials erected to Abu Khdeir on the spot of his immolation.

The international community typically sees the manifestations of Israel's violent racism only when they erupt as assaults on the Gaza Strip, the West Bank, or Lebanon. But Israel's increasingly poisonous anti-Arab and anti-Muslim public culture prepares the ground of domestic public opinion long before any military operation and immunizes the army from most criticism of its "excesses." Moreover, Israeli anti-democratic and racist sentiment is increasingly directed against Palestinian citizens of Israel, who comprise twenty percent of the population.

Foreign Minister Avigdor Lieberman of the Yisrael Beytenu (Israel Is Our Home) Party made his political reputation on the slogan "No

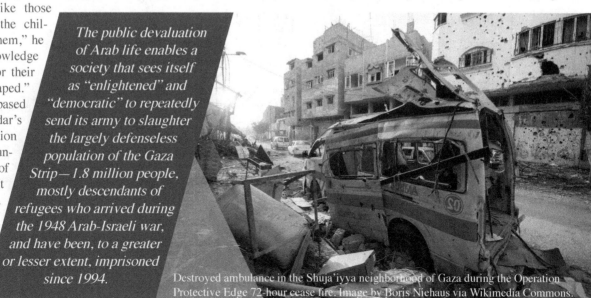

The public devaluation of Arab life enables a society that sees itself as "enlightened" and "democratic" to repeatedly send its army to slaughter the largely defenseless population of the Gaza Strip—1.8 million people, mostly descendants of refugees who arrived during the 1948 Arab-Israeli war, and have been, to a greater or lesser extent, imprisoned since 1994.

Destroyed ambulance in the Shuja'iyya neighborhood of Gaza during the Operation Protective Edge 72-hour cease fire. Image by Boris Niehaus via Wikimedia Commons.

Loyalty, No Citizenship"—a demand that Palestinian Israelis swear loyalty oaths as a condition of retaining their citizenship. Since 2004 Lieberman has also advocated "transferring" Palestinian-Israelis residing in the Triangle region to a future Palestinian state, while annexing most West Bank settlements to Israel. In November 2011 *Haaretz* published a partial list of ten "loyalty-citizenship" bills in various stages of legislation designed to "determine certain citizens' rights according to their 'loyalty' to the state."

While Lieberman and other MKs pursue legal channels to legally undermine the citizenship of Palestinian-Israelis, their civil rights are already in serious danger. In 2010 eighteen local rabbis warned that the Galilee town of Safed faced an "Arab takeover" and instructed Jewish residents to inform on and boycott Jews who sold or rented dwellings to Arabs. In addition to promoting segregated housing, Safed's chief rabbi, Shmuel Eliyahu, tried to ban Arab students from attending Safed Academic College (about 1,300 Palestinian-Israelis are enrolled, some of whom live in Safed). The rabbinical statement incited rampages by religious Jews chanting "Death to the Arabs," leading *Haaretz* columnist Gideon Levy to dub Safed "the most racist city" in Israel. In Karmiel and Upper Nazareth—towns established as part of Israel's campaign to "Judaize the Galilee"—elected officials have led similar campaigns.

Palestinian Israeli Knesset members receive regular verbal abuse from their Jewish "colleagues." For example, Hanin Zoabi (National Democratic Alliance), who participated in the 2010 Freedom Flotilla to the Gaza Strip, which Israeli naval commandos attacked, killing nine Turks (one of whom also held US citizenship), has been particularly targeted. In the verbal sparring over the murder of the three teens Foreign Minister Lieberman called her a "terrorist." Not to be outdone, Miri Regev (Likud) said Zoabi should be "expelled to Gaza and stripped of her [Knesset] immunity." Other Knesset members—some from putatively "liberal" parties—piled on. [Update: 29 July—Hanin Zoabi was suspended from Knesset].

Violence against Arabs in and around Israeli-annexed "Greater Jerusalem" is particularly intense. Much of it is the work of Orthodox Jews. The Jewish Defense League, banned in Israel in 1994 and designated a terrorist organization by the FBI in 2001, and several similar groups regularly assault and harass Arabs. The day of the funeral of the three abducted teens, some two hundred Israelis rampaged through the streets of Jerusalem chanting "Death to Arabs." The previous evening, hardcore fans of the Betar Jerusalem football club, known as La Familia, rallied chanting "Death to the Arabs." The same chant is frequently heard at games of the team, which is associated with the Likud and does not hire Arab players. Hate marches, beatings and shootings of Arabs, and destruction of their property, long common in the West Bank, have become regular events in Israel-proper in the last month.

The citizenship-loyalty bills, Safed's designation as "the most racist city," the attacks volleyed at Palestinian elected officials, and mob violence against Arabs all took place before Israel launched Operation Protective Edge on 8 July. The operation—more aggressively dubbed "Firm Cliff" in Hebrew—constitutes Israel's third assault on the Gaza Strip since 2008. As of yesterday, 29 July, the Palestinian death toll in that operation has reached over 1,200, the great majority of them civilians. Thirty-two Israeli soldiers and three civilians have also died. Israeli security officials sardonically call these operations "mowing the lawn" because well-informed observers know that Hamas cannot be uprooted and is capable of rebuilding its military capacity. There is no long-term strategy, except, as Gideon Levy put it, to kill Palestinians. Major General (res.) Oren Shachor elaborated, "If we kill their families, that will frighten them." And what might deter Israel?

[This piece originally appeared in a special weeklong series on the Stanford University Press blog, and is reposted here in partnership with SUP blog. The entire ten-part series can be found on the SUP blog.]

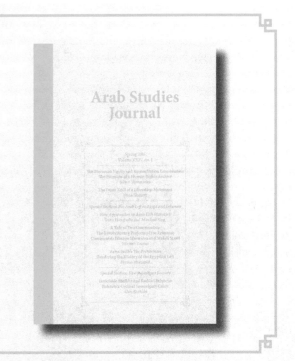

Israel Will Invade Gaza Again... The Only Question is How Soon

Noura Erakat One year ago today, Israel began its fifty-one-day aerial and ground offensive against the besieged population of the Gaza Strip. During the military campaign, Israel concentrated the population into the center of the territory, thus exacerbating its severe density; sealed the borders; launched more than six thousand airstrikes; and fired almost fifty thousand artillery and tank shells. Under these circumstances, the results could only be devastating—and they were. The offensive killed 2,251 Palestinians, including 551 children; communities were devastated, with 142 families losing three or more members; more than 1,500 children were orphaned; more than 150,000 homes as well as 140 schools were partially or completely destroyed; and 373,000 traumatized children were left in need of psycho-social treatment.

The intervening year has brought little relief to the people of Gaza. Not a single home that was destroyed has been rebuilt, the siege remains intact, and eighty percent of the population is dependent on some form of aid for survival. Yet, amid the instability, Palestinians in Gaza can count on one certainty: last summer's onslaught of the Gaza Strip will be repeated with similar or greater force.

Despite the ferocity of Operation Protective Edge (Israel's name for the onslaught), the destruction of the coastal enclave, home to nearly two million Palestinians, was not an exceptional policy in the face of exceptional circumstances. It is Israel's official policy toward the Gaza Strip, and a particularly brutal extension of its broader policy toward all Palestinians.

Israel's policies toward Palestinians are built on a set of twin axioms: to obtain the maximum amount of Palestinian land with the minimum number of Palestinian people and to concentrate a maximum number of Palestinians onto a minimum amount of land. Israel removes, dispossesses, and concentrates Palestinians throughout Israel and the Occupied Territories regardless of their geographic residence or legal jurisdiction. It does so by martial law in the West Bank, by a mix of martial and administrative law in East Jerusalem, and by civil law in Israel. In the Gaza Strip, it does this by siege and warfare.

Israel explains its crippling siege and devastating attacks on Gaza as necessary responses to Hamas rocket fire. In this scenario, Hamas is the powerful aggressor, and there would be no conflict without it. Yet this claim does not withstand empirical and historical evidence.

Gaza, once a city-district of historic Palestine and now a "Strip," sits on the eastern coast of the Mediterranean Sea. Its harbor and fertile land has made it a focal point of trade and empire for centuries, including for the Romans, Napoleon's France, the Mongols, and now Israel. Prior to 1948, the Gaza district contained almost ninety towns and villages. It was thirty-eight times larger than the current Strip, making it the largest district in Mandatory Palestine (the name for the territory during the period of British rule, after World War I), until Zionist militias destroyed a majority of these towns. Upon Israel's establishment, a truncated Gaza absorbed nearly twenty-five percent of Palestinian refugees exiled from their former homes, increasing the enclave's population from eighty thousand to 280,000. That number has grown to 1.8 million today, making Gaza one of the most densely populated places in the world.

From the end of the 1948 war until the war of 1967, Gaza was ruled by Gamal Abdel Nasser's Egypt. It was during this time that the Gaza Strip became a "hotbed of Palestinian nationalism," in the words of French academic Jean-Pierre Filiu, and a site of resistance to Israeli settler-colonialism. Filiu continues that Israel "became obsessed with the menace from Gaza."

Palestinians in Gaza can count on one certainty: last summer's onslaught of the Gaza Strip will be repeated with similar or greater force.

Israel first tried to occupy the Gaza Strip in 1956, during the Sinai War, but was forced to withdraw its troops under intense US pressure after only four months. Just a decade later, during the war of 1967, it occupied Gaza more successfully and immediately began to integrate Gaza's water system and electricity grid into Israel's own. Hamas was nowhere in existence when Israel staged both of these invasions. In fact, when Sheikh Ahmed Yassin established the precursor to Hamas as an offshoot of the Muslim Brotherhood in 1973, Israel tolerated it because it viewed the organization as an effective counterweight to the far more popular Fatah and the Palestine Liberation Organization (PLO). Hamas was not established as an Islamic-nationalist resistance movement until 1988, and it did not launch its first armed attack until early 1989, when it captured and killed two Israeli soldiers.

In 1991, Israel entered into the Madrid Peace Conference, the negotiations with the PLO that preceded the Oslo Accords. In preparation for incremental withdrawal stipulated by the Oslo agreement, Israel accelerated its isolation, containment, and systematic de-development of the Gaza Strip. It did so in order

Dar al-Fadila Association for Orphans was destroyed during the Israeli assault on Gaza. Image from user ISM Palestine via Flickr.

to separate Gaza from the broader Palestinian-Israeli conflict and to ensure control over the territory under any ensuing permanent arrangement. Israel began importing foreign labor to replace its Palestinian labor force, which had performed much of Israel's most grinding and lowest paid work.

Israel's policies toward Palestinians are built on a set of twin axioms: to obtain the maximum amount of Palestinian land with the minimum number of Palestinian people and to concentrate a maximum number of Palestinians onto a minimum amount of land.

This was the beginning of a particularly challenging period for the people of Gaza. At the end of the Gulf War, in February 1991, Kuwait evicted Palestinians in retaliation for Yasir Arafat's support of Iraq's occupation. This caused a complete halt in remittances, estimated at 120 million dollars in 1989, to Palestinians in the Occupied Territories. Together with the fact that Gaza no longer had an export market for its produce in the Gulf, the economic downturn was severe. The number of Palestinian families receiving food aid rose from roughly ten thousand in June 1990 to 120,000 by June 1991, and Gaza's gross national product fell by forty-one percent. Significantly,

by 1993, the number of people who depended on aid from the United Nations Relief and Works Agency for Palestine Refugees, the primary humanitarian organization for Palestinian refugees around the world, had stabilized at eighty thousand. By the end of Operation Protective Edge, that number skyrocketed to 830,000.

The years leading up to 1991 also marked the period of the first intifada, the popular, and largely nonviolent, Palestinian uprising (the intifada began in late 1987). Palestinians engaged in civil disobedience, general strikes, economic boycotts, and resistance economies, as well as the throwing of stones and Molotov cocktails. But Hamas had still yet to launch a single suicide attack on Israeli civilians when, in March 1993, Israel initiated its closure policy of both the West Bank and Gaza (encircling Gaza behind an actual fence), which controlled the movement of people and goods within and between the noncontiguous territories. In instances of "total closure," it prevented all entry and exit by Palestinians from the territories. With the borders now fully controlled by Israel, the Gazan economy became completely dependent on Israel and incapable of self-sustenance. Nine months later, Israel and the PLO signed the Oslo Accords. Shortly after that, then-Foreign Minister Shimon Peres told a UNESCO conference that he saw the Gaza Strip progressively evolving into a Palestinian state, while the West Bank would become an autonomous polity of Palestinians and Israeli settlers whose status and borders would eventually be defined.

By the eve of 1994, Israel had sealed Gaza, set it on a course of de-development, and set it apart from the broader conflict with the intent of establishing it as the Palestinian micro-state—all before Hamas launched a single suicide attack or mortar into Israel.

Hamas launched its first suicide attack on 6 April 1994, in retaliation for the murder of twenty-nine Palestinians praying in the Ibrahimi mosque in Hebron. In 2000, during the start of the second intifada, Israel declared that it was now engaged in an "armed conflict short of war" in the occupied West Bank and the Gaza Strip and deployed unprecedented military force against Palestinians, including aerial bombardments and airborne extrajudicial assassinations, also known as targeted killings. In this context, Hamas launched its first rocket into Israel in March 2001.

Insisting that Hamas rocket fire explains Israel's engagement with Palestinians in Gaza does not adequately explain Israel's decades-long policies toward the coastal enclave.

In April 2004, then-Prime Minister Ariel Sharon publicly announced his plan for unilateral disengagement from Gaza in exchange for consolidation and control of settlements in the West Bank, thus setting in accelerated motion Peres's vision for Palestinian statehood articulated in his UNESCO speech. Sharon's senior adviser, Dov Weisglass, explained that the disengagement was meant to freeze the peace process by supplying "the amount of formaldehyde that is necessary so there will not be a political process with the Palestinians." The idea was that unilateral withdrawal would alter the balance of power by offering a veneer of Palestinian independence without relinquishing Israeli control.

To prepare for disengagement, Israel embarked on a series of military campaigns that continue to the present day. Israel launched the first campaigns in April 2004, a little more than a year before the disengagement in August and September 2005, with the aim of expanding the northern and southern buffer zones between the Gaza Strip and Israel.

Since disengagement, Israel has declared several all out wars against the Gaza Strip. It tightened its siege in January 2006, when Hamas won parliamentary elections in Gaza, and declared Gaza a "hostile entity" in September 2007, after Hamas routed Fatah from the Gaza Strip in response to a US-backed preemptive coup. Upon Hamas's assumption of power in Gaza, Israel, together with the United States and the European Union, imposed the most severe form of a naval blockade and land siege experienced by Palestinians in Gaza. The siege together with Israeli military campaigns ushered a humanitarian crisis in the Gaza Strip, and it is in this context that Palestinians began building a tunnel network to survive, and resist, the blockade.

Hostilities between Hamas and Israel continued during this time until Egypt negotiated a cease-fire in June 2008. After just four months, Israel broke that cease-fire, thus triggering Operation Cast Lead, which lasted for twenty-two days, from 27 December 2008, until 18 January 2009. Israeli forces killed some 1,400 Palestinians, including more than three hundred children, and injured approximately 4,300 others, including 1,100 children. They also destroyed 2,900 homes, twenty-nine schools, 121 commercial and industrial workshops, sixty police stations, and thirty mosques. Significantly, the Israeli defense minister at the time, Ehud Barak, had begun planning Cast Lead long before he helped launch it, some six months before, as Israel was beginning to negotiate the June 2008 ceasefire.

Israel and Hamas then entered into another cease-fire that Israel disrupted when it assassinated Ahmed al-Jabari in November 2012; Jabari was the designated diplomat representing Hamas in negotiations with Israel. This assassination triggered Israel's second large-scale military offensive since 2008, Operation Pillar of Cloud, which killed 177 Palestinians and injured approximately 1,500 others in eight days. The operation launched one year ago, on 7 July 2014, which Israel provoked, is a continuation of these policies and worse than any of its predecessors.

Insisting that Hamas rocket fire explains Israel's engagement with Palestinians in Gaza does not adequately explain Israel's decades-long policies toward the coastal enclave. It also does not explain Israel's policies toward Palestinians in the West Bank, including East Jerusalem, or within Israel who continue to endure removal, dispossession, and containment despite the lack of rockets from there.

Israel's policies toward Gaza are an extension of its ambitions to remove and replace Palestinians living on their historic lands. The cessation of this violence requires a comprehensive political solution that grapples with the settler-colonial conditions endured by all Palestinians.

At this point Israelis and Palestinians are in a holding pattern. The question is for how long? The World Health Organization predicts that, due to siege and warfare, the Gaza Strip will be unlivable by 2020. Given Israel's destruction of Gaza's tunnel networks in the summer of 2014, its only lifeline since 2007, relief from this intensifying humanitarian catastrophe is nearly impossible without ending the siege. Therefore, as far as some Palestinians are concerned, they will either die quietly at the hands of these cruel policies or die in front of cameras militarily resisting these conditions. Under the present circumstances, the premature death of Palestinians in the Gaza Strip is inevitable.

Responsibility for altering this course belongs to all of us—individuals, organizations, and states. The status quo in the Gaza Strip today is a function of human-made politics, not natural disasters, and it will take human-made solutions, captured in a series of political choices and formative junctures, to upend the status quo and alter this daunting calculus.

In Jerusalem, "Religious War" Claims Cloak Old-Fashioned Colonialism

Israeli police outside the Dome of the Rock. Image from user Crazymaq via Flickr.

Nur Arafeh

Al-Shabaka Policy Brief Overview

The escalating clashes between Israeli settlers and Jerusalemite Palestinians are the harbingers of a major eruption with incalculable consequences. Immediately billed as a "religious war" by the media and Israeli right wingers, they are in fact the outcome of longstanding Israeli plans to Judaize the city and empty it of its Palestinian inhabitants. Al-Shabaka Policy member Nur Arafeh analyzes the major changes that Israel has illegally imposed on Jerusalem and addresses the Palestine Liberation Organization/Palestinian Authority's effective abandonment of the population to fend for itself. She concludes with policy recommendations to the PLO/PA, Palestinian academics and analysts, and the international solidarity movement.

The Myth of Religious War

Jerusalem has been thrust into the spotlight due to the recent clashes between Israeli settlers and Palestinians at the al-Aqsa Mosque. Also referred to as al-Haram al-Sharif or the Noble Sanctuary, the compound contains al-Aqsa itself, Islam's third holiest site, and the Dome of the Rock, where Prophet Muhammad is said to have ascended to heaven. Jews revere the site in the belief that it was once the location of two ancient Jewish temples.

> *The framing of these events as a religious war not only ignores the reality of the power imbalance between the colonizer and the colonized, but also fails to address the history and context in which the recent events have unfolded.*

A number of ultra-Orthodox Jews have been repeatedly violating the status quo that has been in place since 1967 by making incursions inside the al-Aqsa compound and calling for Israel to build a third temple on what they term the Temple Mount.[1] A video posted recently on YouTube by the Temple Institute, which is part of the so-called Temple Mount and Land of Israel Faithful Movement, depicts a third temple replacing al-Aqsa Mosque and the Dome of the Rock.

The recent clashes between Palestinians and Israeli settlers and police in Jerusalem were punctuated by horrific attacks like the kidnapping and murder of the Palestinian youth, Mohammad Abu-Khdeir in July 2014. After Yehuda Glick, a key figure in the Temple Institute and a strong advocate of its messianic scheme, was allegedly shot by a Palestinian, members of the Temple Mount Movement made further incursions into al-Aqsa, and on 30 October 2014 Israel banned prayers in the compound for the first time since 1967. Tensions in Jerusalem reached boiling point after an attack by two Palestinians on an ultra-orthodox synagogue on 18 November 2014 left four Jews and a Druze police officer dead. The New Year began with a warning by the Mufti of Jerusalem of an Israeli organization's plans to register al-Aqsa Mosque as Israeli property.

But can this really be described as the start of a religious war? Has the political conflict indeed been transformed into a war of beliefs? According to *The Guardian*: "This is what a religious war looks like." A Palestinian *Al-Hiwar* commentator agreed. Deputy Knesset Member Moshe Feiglin went even further and described it as a global fight "against the evil forces of the most extreme Islam." Worse, the Temple Mount Movement stands reality on its head by proclaiming that one of its long-term objectives is to "liberate the Temple Mount from Arab (Islamic) occupation," thus portraying the colonizers as the colonized.

Yet the framing of these events as a religious war not only ignores the reality of the power imbalance between the colonizer and the colonized, but also fails to address the history and context in which the recent events have unfolded.

Israel's Longstanding Targeting of Al-Aqsa Mosque

Jewish religious law prohibits Jews from praying in the al-Aqsa compound; Jews are only expected to revere the site, but not to visit or own it for fear of profaning the inner sanctum of the alleged temple, and are to pray at al-Buraq Wall (renamed the Western Wall). Nevertheless, extremists have early on targeted al-Aqsa Mosque with a view to rebuilding the temple. In 1982, Meir Kahane, leader of the far-right Kach party, marched on the compound holding plans of the temple to be built on the ruins of al-Aqsa. In 1990, twenty-one Palestinians were killed and 150 were injured in clashes with members of the Temple Mount Movement who attempted to enter al-Aqsa and place the foundation stone for the temple. In 1996, Israeli excavations and the digging of tunnels near al-Aqsa sparked violence that resulted in the killing of seventy Palestinians and fifteen Israeli soldiers.

The Israeli government has also been supporting efforts to ensure Jewish control over the compound. Almost half of Likud party members support the Temple Mount Movement, which has recently won funding from the government. Between 2008 and 2011, the Temple Institute received an annual donation of 107,000 dollars from the Ministry of Education and the Ministry of Culture, Science and Sports. In 2012, an educational unit in the Temple Institute was offered an additional fifty thousand dollars from the Ministry of Education.

However, the actions of specific groups to take control of al-Aqsa should not be seen as isolated incidents, but rather as part of a larger Zionist project to Judaize Jerusalem and ensure Jewish supremacy over the city.

Creation of a New Reality in Jerusalem

Since the occupation began in 1967, Israel has been committed to transforming a multi-religious and multi-cultural city into a "reunified" Jewish city under the exclusive control and sovereignty of Israel. It has fast-tracked the Judaization of the city via policies that impact on the geographical and physical space and are designed to circumvent the "demographic threat" posed by Palestinians.

From the outset in 1967, Israel illegally annexed seventy square kilometers of West Bank territory, including East Jerusalem (6.5km2), such that it maximized the area of land expropriated while minimizing the number of Palestinians. It also razed the Arab neighborhoods of Bab al-Magharbeh and Harat al-Sharaf to build the Jewish Quarter, al-Buraq Wall plaza, houses for settlers, and Jewish synagogues. Israel also reshaped the physical landscape of Jerusalem by constructing a ring of settlements around the city, linked to bypass roads to ensure geographic continuity with other Israeli settlements in the West Bank.[2]

The ensuing physical and political fragmentation of Jerusalem went hand in hand with its economic isolation long before Israel embarked on the construction of the Apartheid Wall in 2002, which redrew the borders away from the pre-1967 armistice line. The construction of the wall was deliberately designed to cut inside the city and exclude areas populated by Palestinians as a means to ensure a Jewish majority.

To deal with the "demographic threat" posed by Palestinians, Israel designated Palestinians living in Jerusalem as "permanent residents"—a civil status usually reserved for foreign citizens and which does not guarantee residency rights. On this basis, resident IDs are often revoked. Between 1967 and 2013, Israel revoked the ID cards of more than 14,309 Palestinian residents. According to the 2003 *Temporary Amendment to the Citizenship and Entry into Israel Law* (amended in 2005 and 2007), West Bank Palestin-

ians married to Jerusalem residents do not qualify for residency status and are only granted temporary permits in exceptional circumstances. In contrast, Jews who immigrate to live in Jerusalem are granted immediate citizenship, reflecting the apartheid nature of the Israeli regime.

The actions of specific groups to take control of al-Aqsa should not be seen as isolated incidents, but rather as part of a larger Zionist project to Judaize Jerusalem and ensure Jewish supremacy over the city.

While strengthening the Jewish presence in Jerusalem, Israel has sought to contain the urban and demographic expansion of Palestinians via discriminatory urban and zoning policies consistent with ethnic cleansing. More than one third of land in Palestinian neighborhoods has been classified as "open landscape areas" where building is prohibited, constricting Palestinian building to only fourteen percent of the land of East Jerusalem and causing an acute housing crisis. Moreover, since 1967, Israel has destroyed 1,673 housing units, affecting around eight thousand people between 1967 and 2013. With the implementation of all these policies, Israel is aiming to achieve a ratio of thirty percent "Arabs" and seventy percent Jews within the Jerusalem municipality.

Discriminatory Israeli policies are also apparent in the discrepancies in service provision between Palestinian and Jewish neighborhoods. Less than ten percent of the municipal budget is allocated to Palestinian districts despite Palestinians paying the same amount of arnona tax as Jewish citizens.

Judaization has been accompanied by "de-Palestinianization" to eradicate the Palestinian identity in Jerusalem. For example, Sultan Suleiman al-Qanuni Street (a sultan of the Ottoman Empire) was renamed King Solomon street and the Wadi Hilweh district of Silwan was renamed "the city of David." Furthermore, unnamed streets in Palestinian areas were recently given Arabic names that are devoid of political and national connotations. This renaming process is linked to the re-writing of history in line with Zionist dicta, a process in which archeology and excavations are exploited to create a fictitious Jewish history of the city, while the heritage of other eras is ignored.

Israeli control over the historical narrative extends to the educational system. Since March 2011 Israel has attempted to force Palestinian schools that receive budget allocations from the Israeli authorities to use textbooks prepared by the Jerusalem Education Administration (so far, five have done so). These books present Palestinian students with a one-sided history and censor any topic related to Palestinian identity and heritage.

Palestinian institutions in Jerusalem have also been targeted to erode Palestinian activism in the city. Since 2001 Israel has closed at least thirty-one Palestinian institutions, including the Orient House, the former headquarters of the PLO, and the Chamber of Commerce and Industry. This climate of repression led many institutions to relocate from Jerusalem and caused a huge institutional vacuum, accompanied by an absence of leadership.

Other steps to de-Palestinianize Jerusalem include the latest five-year socio-economic "development" plan for Palestinian areas approved in June 2014 by the Israeli cabinet. This plan focuses on gaps in infrastructure, education, social welfare, and employment between Palestinian and Jewish neighborhoods in an apparent attempt to encourage the integration of Palestinians within Israel and bolster security by thwarting "violence" and "stone throwing."

In other words, development is a tool to strengthen Israeli control over Jerusalem and suppress Palestinian steadfastness and resistance to the Israeli occupation. Thus, the plan cannot be seen as an initiative to address the deteriorating socio-economic conditions of Palestinians in Jerusalem in terms of the extremely high poverty rate (seventy-five percent of Palestinian residents live below the Israeli definition of the poverty line); collapsing trade and tourism sectors; lack of investment; depleted health and educational services; high unemployment rates (16.7 percent in 2014); and high costs of living.

In this context, Palestinian clashes with Israeli Jews should be seen as acts of resistance and desperation within the larger historical struggle of Palestinians against occupation, apartheid, ethnic cleansing, land theft, dispossession, forced displacement, and economic marginalization. The recent intensification of incursions at al-Aqsa and calls to build a third temple simply ignited the flames of these smoldering emotions. To focus on the religious dimensions of the recent unrest while overlooking its root causes would only lead to further violent clashes and eruptions of unprecedented magnitude. Religion is being exploited to serve Israeli political and national goals as it entrenches its colonial apartheid policies.

The Leadership Vacuum Leaves Palestinians Powerless

The recent unrest in Jerusalem, in which Palestinians have resorted to new forms of resistance such as vehicles and fireworks, should be seen within the broader context of a city that lacks political leadership. The Palestinian Authority (PA) has demonstrated a lack of genuine investment in Jerusalem since signing the 1993 Oslo Declaration of Principles, of which the PA was itself a product. This was already evident when the Palestine Liberation Organization (PLO) accepted to defer the issue of Jerusalem to the negotiations on the final status of the occupied Palestinian territory (OPT). While the PLO/PA clings tightly to the farcical peace process, Israel has entrenched its occupation and control over Jerusalem.

In a clear divergence from its rhetoric of support, the PA allocates a negligible budget to the city. The total budget allocated to the Ministry of Jerusalem Affairs and to the Jerusalem Governorate was around fifteen million dollars in 2014, representing 0.4 percent of the total PA budget expenditure for that year. Compare this shameful and insignificant budget allocation to the supposed capital of the Palestinian state with the twenty-seven percent of the budget allocated to the security sector in the same year. Moreover, most of the budget is disbursed in the areas of Jerusalem that fall under Palestinian administration and outside the wall. Locations such as Shu'fat and Beit Hanina that lie within the Israeli municipal boundaries of Jerusalem rarely receive any funds.[3]

This meager budget is the main reason that prompted Hatem Abdel-Qader to resign forty days after his appointment as the first minister for Jerusalem affairs in 2009. He noted that the Palestinian "government fails to uphold its commitments to the city, which is undergoing a difficult period." Another Palestinian intellectual, who served as a PA representative in Jerusalem, also argued that, "The PA's behavior was never in line with its stated goals. It has continuously failed to implement the numerous studies and plans made for the city."[4]

While Israel is turning its vision for Jerusalem into reality via numerous policies and master plans (2020, 2030 and 2050), a coherent strategy for the future of the city by the Palestinian leadership remains absent. This was apparent in the omission of a development plan for Jerusalem in the *National Development Plan 2014-2016*. Although it is true that the document refers back to the *Strategic Multi-Sector Development Plan for East Jerusalem (SMDP) 2011-2013* issued by the Jerusalem Unit at the President's Office, the SMDP was published in 2010 and requires updating. Moreover, the Jerusalem Unit itself, which was previously allocated most of the funds for Jerusalem, was closed in 2010.[5]

> *Religion is being exploited to serve Israeli political and national goals as it entrenches its colonial apartheid policies.*

More significantly, the development approach used in the SMDP disconnects development from political and colonial realities; it reduces Palestinian struggle to that of "survival" instead of freedom, and takes the Israeli occupation as given rather than seeking to end it. As the introductory section of the SMDP put it: "How can the PLO assist Jerusalemites to *survive* and thrive *within the existing context* in order to have a solid foundation for the capital of the future Palestinian state?" (emphasis added).

The lack of genuine official interest in the city, the emergence of Ramallah as the de facto capital, and the absence of Palestinian political leadership in Jerusalem, leave Palestinians feeling abandoned and resentful towards the PLO/PA. PA President Mahmoud Abbas is still paying lip service to Palestinians in Jerusalem, while refusing to end security collaboration with Israel or to support non-violent means of resistance such as the boycott of *all* Israeli goods.

Meanwhile, Israel has responded to leaderless Palestinian protests and resistance with characteristic force that includes land confiscation, house demolitions, and collective punishment, such as raids on homes, spraying neighborhoods with putrid water, and mass arrests. For example, between June and September, approximately seven hundred Palestinians were arrested in Jerusalem, the majority of them children, according to al-Dameer Association for Human Rights.[6] Israeli settlers who commit brutal crimes against Palestinians undergo no such punishment. In fact, the Israeli government has eased gun restrictions and increased funding to protect settlers in Jerusalem, additional evidence of the institutionalized discrimination to which Palestinians are subjected.

Protecting Jerusalem and Its Palestinians

The current turmoil in Jerusalem is the result of colonial subjugation, institutionalized discrimination, dispossession, and Israel's establishment of facts on the ground to ensure it maintains Jewish supremacy over the city. Israel's plans should thus be resisted locally and internationally, primarily by increasing their cost to Israel. The apartheid system in South Africa only began to unravel once the costs of preserving white supremacy became too high to bear.

First and foremost, Palestinians need proactive leadership that will propel the status of Jerusalem to the forefront of government commitment and to the heart of the national struggle as a matter of urgency. It is vital that Palestinians project a clear vision of Jerusalem to counter the prevailing Israeli vision. Information and communication are key tools to counter Israel's re-writing of history and silencing of the Palestinian narrative.

In particular, Palestinian leadership should confront Israeli attempts to frame its colonial policies in religious terms and should remind the world that the core issues are those of occupation, dispossession, and land theft. It is imperative to challenge the power of the Israeli discourse by exposing its shameful record of oppression in Jerusalem and the rest of the occupied territory. The PLO/PA should also further capitalize on the hard won status in international organizations such as UNESCO to take legal steps to protect al-Aqsa and the Old City in Jerusalem.

Secondly, academics and policy analysts can play a crucial role in putting Jerusalem in the vanguard. To date, Palestinian intellectuals have been biased towards the analysis of socio-economic development in the West Bank, and, to some extent, the Gaza Strip, to the detriment of discussion about Jerusalem. Palestinians must emphasize Jerusalem in their discourse and move beyond mere diagnosis of problems to devise solutions. The concept of development under occupation itself needs to be revised and redefined as a form of economic, political, and social resistance embedded in the larger historical struggle of Palestinians for self-determination, freedom, and justice.

Finally, the local boycott of Israeli goods and services is a vital means of resisting the Israeli occupation. Not only is it a moral duty for every Palestinian but also the boycott of Israeli products increases the cost of Israel's apartheid system and enhances the productive capacity of the Palestinian economy. In parallel, thought must be given to ways to develop a Palestinian economy capable of resisting integration and dependence on the Israeli economy and that can pave the foundations for a solid political base from which an emancipated and self-determining society may emerge.

At the international level, the Palestinian-led Boycott, Divestment, and Sanctions (BDS) movement, and the pressure this imposes on Israel worldwide should be maintained and intensified. Arab countries need to engage in a significant way to isolate Israel for its designs on Jerusalem and its multiple human rights violations.

Without concerted efforts by Palestinians with Arab and international support to uphold Palestinian rights in Jerusalem, the present small fires in the city could turn into a conflagration with permanent damage to Palestinian and Arab heritage in the city and to the Palestinian Jerusalemite presence in the city of their ancestors.

[This article was originally published on al-shabaka.org]

Endnotes:

1. Following Israel's occupation and illegal annexation of East Jerusalem in 1967, the control of the mosque and Noble Sanctuary were transferred to a Jordanian Islamic waqf (trust). The 1994 Wadi Araba agreement between Jordan and Israel stipulated Jordan's guardianship over all Muslim holy shrines in Jerusalem.
2. Two plans were drafted specifically for this purpose: The Greater Jerusalem Project intended to create a "greater Jerusalem" extending over an area of six hundred square kilometers; and the E1 plan called for the expansion of Ma'ale Adumim settlement to ensure its connection with Jerusalem. Both plans would cause geographical discontinuity between the northern and southern parts of the West Bank, and would further isolate the eastern part of Jerusalem from the rest of the occupied Palestinian territory.
3. Author's interview.
4. Unless otherwise stated, all quotes come from interviews conducted by the author in November and December 2014.
5. Author's interview.
6. Author's interview.

KNOWLEDGE PRODUCTION PROJECT

LAUNCHING NOVEMBER 2016

JADMAG PEDAGOGY PUBLICATIONS ISSUE 4.1

Permission to Kill in Gaza

Noura Erakat

In the summer of 2014, Israel un-leashed unprecedented violence against the Gaza Strip. Although it was the third such large-scale attack since 2008, the fourteenth military offensive since Israel's unilateral disengagement in 2005, and the twenty-second since former Prime Minister Ariel Sharon announced plans for disengagement in April 2004, Operation Protective Edge (OPE) was by far more violent and merciless than any of its predecessors. In large part, this shift reflected Israel's radical innovations in the laws of war with the aim of expanding its right to use force and to diminish protections for Palestinian civilians. These in-novations—which defy and deviate from international consensus about the legal rights of states—reflect a move that Israel set in motion at the beginning of the second Palestinian intifada in 2000 and accelerated following its unilateral withdrawal from Gaza in 2005. The use of force against Gaza in 2014 reflects a new norm that Israel, together with the United States, aims to establish in the context of counter-terrorism operations. This "new normal" means that future confrontations between Israel and Palestinian combatants, as well as Hizballah for that matter, will likely entail similar shows of devastating force.

Damaged UN school and remnants of the Ministry of Interior in Gaza, Dec. 2012. Image from user Grahaa via Wikimedia Commons

> *Israel has claimed the right to wage war against the population while simultaneously denying combatant status to Palestinian fighters. The denial of such status allowed Israel to criminalize all use of force—including defensive operations and those targeting Israeli soldiers and military objects.*

The scope of death and destruction in Gaza in the summer of 2014 was an inevitable result of this "new normal." Consider that Israel's comprehensive siege, together with the Egyptian regime's collusion to seal the Rafah crossing, meant that Palestinians had nowhere to flee during hostilities. Consider also that the Gaza Strip, 365 square kilometers and home to 1.8 million Palestin-ians, is one of the most densely populated places on earth. During the 2014 attack, Israel expanded the buffer zone from the eastern and northern land borders by forty-four percent, thus further con-centrating the population. With nowhere to flee and concentrated into the center of the Strip, any aerial attack on the Gaza Strip would be an attack on the entire population. These circumstances ensured grotesque devastation upon Gaza's population.

Since the start of the second intifada in September 2000, Israel has insisted that it is engaged in an "armed conflict short of war" with Pales-tinians in the West Bank and Gaza. Following Israel's unilateral disengagement from the Gaza Strip in 2005, the government disingenuously de-clared the cessation of military occupation there, de-spite maintaining its effective control of the territory and terming Gaza a "hostile entity" to denote its lack of sovereignty.

This legal ambiguity has been deployed by Israeli officials to argue that the situation in Gaza is sui generis, and therefore not regulated by traditional laws of armed conflict. Instead, Israel has claimed the right to wage war against the population while simultaneously denying combatant status to Palestinian fighters. The denial of such status allowed Israel to criminal-ize all use of force—including defensive operations and those targeting Israeli soldiers and military objects. Moreover, Israel categorized all fighters in Gaza as civilians who are direct-ly participating in hostilities, rather than as combatants who have the right to kill to achieve a military advantage. As such, Israel denied captured Palestinian fighters the designation as prisoners of war, or POWs. At the same time, Israel accreted to itself the "right" to engage in assassination operations under the cover of war.

> *Israel considers all Hamas-affiliated infrastructure, be it educational, governmental, or medical, to be a legitimate target.*

Until September 2001 the US government publicly rejected Isra-el's attempts to reinterpret the laws of war. Following al-Qaʻida's attacks on the World Trade Center and the Pentagon, however, the Bush administration emulated Israel's novel approach and integrated similar arguments and tactics into the lexicon of the United States' global "war on terror." Those approaches continue to be advanced by the Obama administration in its drone warfare and targeted killing policy. This background helps explain the lack of condemnation of Israel's unprecedented and unlawful rules of engagement in 2014.

Five of Israel's most troubling claims are:

1) No Palestinian Combatants

Israel has insisted that no Palestinians have the status of "combatants" which would entail a right to fight. Instead, all Palestinians who engage in combat are regarded as direct participants in hostilities (DPH). Whereas Article 51(3) of the 1949 Geneva Conventions stipulates that a DPH forfeits his civilian immunity "for such time" as he takes up arms, Israel insists that Palestinian fighters have a continuous combat function. This is applied to mean that they can be targeted at any time and place, even when they are sleeping in a residential complex full of other civilians. Israel also claims that membership in Hamas is sufficient reason to deny Palestinians civilian immunity. This contravenes the principle of distinction, which aims to protect civilians, and purports that only combatants as well as DPHs during the time of their military engagement can be legitimately targeted. Despite the fact that Hamas is a political organization with a military wing, Israel views all Hamas members, political leaders, and indeed anyone on its payroll as legitimate military targets.

> *Since 2005, Israeli legal advisers have advanced the notion that their soldiers' lives are worth more than the lives of enemy civilians. This radical proposition shifts the risk of warfare from soldiers to civilians in its calculus of military advantage in relation to collateral damage.*

In 2008, Israel explicitly defended its attack on a class of eight hundred police cadets because it reasoned that during warfare, these civilian forces would join Hamas's military forces. This is a radical reading of international humanitarian law. The equivalent would be to consider nearly all Israelis aged eighteen or above as legitimate targets because they would be conscripted into the army or called to serve if they were part of its reservist troops. Moreover, it would mean that Hamas could target homes where Israeli army pilots slept at night away from the battlefield.

2) No Civilian Infrastructure

Similarly, Israel considers all Hamas-affiliated infrastructure, be it educational, governmental, or medical, to be a legitimate target. Israel's IDF Law Division explained that it authorized the targeting of Hamas-affiliated buildings because

> ...the way Hamas operates is to use the entire governmental infrastructure for the organization's terrorist purposes, so that the distinctions are a bit different. We adjust the targets to the case of a terrorist regime.

International humanitarian law requires that a belligerent assess, first, whether the infrastructure's purpose is primarily civilian or military in nature; second, whether destruction of that infrastructure has a definitive military advantage; and third, whether that advantage outweighs the civilian harm that would result from an attack. Instead, Israel's assessment was sweeping. It targeted government ministries, schools, electrical grids, and desalination plants. In other cases, it dispensed with proportionality assessments to target an entire apartment complex if so much as a single room was presumed to store weapons. In several instances, this meant targeting infrastructure based on mere speculation of combatant activity. A particularly notorious instance was the targeting of seven UNRWA schools sheltering thousands of Palestinian civilians where no weapons or fighters were present.

Israel considers its military advantage in five-year increments, rather than in terms of the immediate consequences of attacks. This dramatically expands the calculations for the permissible use of force.

---

3) Warning of Impending Attack as a Carte Blanche

By virtue of issuing warnings for impending attacks, Israeli forces acted as if they were relieved of responsibility for civilian casualties. These warnings take the form of leafletting or "knocking on the roof" of a building about to be bombed with a smaller missile. They are, therefore, quite controversial because they foster fear and panic among the civilian population. In law, if a warning is ineffective and the civilian population cannot flee or take shelter, the attacking state maintains a duty to distinguish between civilians and combatants. This is necessary to balance the anticipated harm against the anticipated military advantage. Instead, Israel considered those who did not flee following a warning as involuntary human shields, whom they consider Hamas's victims of "terrorism." Israel has not been clear, however, whether these involuntary human shields constitute civilian harm to be considered in its proportionality assessment. Its military decisions reflect that they did not count: at least 142 families lost three or more members in attacks on residential buildings resulting in at least 742 casualties. Based on their investigation, the International Federation for Human Rights (FIDH) concluded that "rather than minimizing loss of civilian life, Israel's warning policy fomented massive forced displacement and spread confusion and fear among the population."

4) Israeli Soldiers' Lives Are Worth More than the Lives of Palestinian Civilians

Since 2005, Israeli legal advisers have advanced the notion that their soldiers' lives are worth more than the lives of enemy civilians. This radical proposition shifts the risk of warfare from soldiers to civilians in its calculus of military advantage in relation to collateral damage. Two of Israel's military doctrines enshrine this radical view. The Dahiya Doctrine explicitly seeks to inflict devastating violence upon civilian populations—including through the use of indiscriminate force—in an effort to deter future operations. The Hannibal Doctrine encourages soldiers to use indiscriminate force when an Israeli soldier is captured, even if it leads to the killing of the captured soldier, in order to avoid the consequences of negotiating for his release and to deter the capture of soldiers to be used as bargaining chips. This doctrine guided Israeli soldiers in the town of Shujai'ya where they killed sixty-six Palestinians in sixty minutes, and in Rafah where they sealed a 1.5 mile radius and entrapped Palestinians in an aerial bombing campaign for two days resulting in 150 casualties.

> *If not rebuffed legally and politically by other states, Israel's innovations, implemented against Gaza's besieged population, could eventually come to be accepted as custom.*

5) Proportionality Is Forward-Looking

Finally, Israel's analysis of its military advantage is forward looking. Israel considers its military advantage in five-year increments, rather than in terms of the immediate consequences of attacks. This dramatically expands the calculations for the permissible use of force. Similarly, while Israel could not legally target agricultural farmland under a traditional proportionality assessment if there were no attacks launched from there, it claims the "right" to target those lands if they could possibly be used by Hamas and other groups to launch strikes in the next five years. That explains how Israel justified the destruction of 419 businesses, thirty-six fishing boats, forty-two thousand acres of farmland, and exacerbated Gaza's unemployment rate which was forty-five percent before the start of this most recent offensive and seventy percent among youth aged twenty to twenty-four.

As grotesque as they may seem, these policies put forward by Israel are not necessarily illegal. That is because the laws of war are established by treaty as well as by custom. Custom is comprised of state practice and opinio juris, or what states deem to be legal. That means that what states do in practice, even if contrary to established treaty-based law, can become custom-

ary law. In the course of its practice, Israel is proposing these are necessary amendments to existing laws of war in order to meet the challenges of modern warfare characterized by irregular combat. Israel is explicitly trying to change the laws of war. Daniel Reisner, the head of Israel's IDF Legal Division until 2004, explains

International law progresses through violations. We invented the targeted assassination thesis and we had to push it. At first there were protrusions that made it hard to insert easily into the legal moulds. Eight years later it is in the center of the bounds of legitimacy.

If not rebuffed legally and politically by other states, Israel's innovations, implemented against Gaza's besieged population, could eventually come to be accepted as custom. The United Nations initiated two investigations, the Commission of Inquiry into Operation Protective Edge writ large and its Board of Inquiry into Israel's attacks on seven UNRWA schools. Both reports have raised serious questions about Israel's practices, but that will mean nothing if the reports are ignored by governments and advocates. Political action is necessary to make the reports' findings meaningful, otherwise they can be marginalized and forgotten. In light of such minimal protest at the top diplomatic levels, it is likely that Israel, together with US military forces, will continue trying to assert these practices as the "new normal" in asymmetric warfare. In fact, in its newly released Law of War Manual, the US Department of State explicitly makes some of these propositions. That means what we witnessed in Gaza in summer 2014 can be repeated and may not even be the worst of what is yet to come.

The Beginning of the End of Palestinian Security Coordination with Israel?

Two Palestinian police standing in front of the Church of the Nativity. Image by James Emery via Wikimedia Commons.

Tariq Dana

While Mahmoud Abbas's infamous speech at the conference of the Organization of Islamic Cooperation has sparked widespread condemnation and outrage among Palestinians, it has also provoked renewed questioning of the increasingly suspicious role of the Palestinian Authority's (PA) security sector. In his speech, Abbas defended security coordination with Israel under any and all circumstances, claiming that such coordination is a "Palestinian national interest." Meanwhile, he had previously characterized it as "sacred."

Criticism of the PA's security coordination with Israel is not new, but recent events demonstrate the egregiousness of the double standard: warm ties with Israeli security set against an iron hand with its people. As a result, a range of voices—men and women, political dissidents and reformers, former prisoners and militants, activists and journalists—have put forward unprecedented criticisms and condemnations of the PA and its security forces. Indeed, for a large segment of the Palestinians, the PA security sector is now viewed as an extension of the occupation. In reaction to the PA's actions, critics now regularly level charges of treason and betrayal.

The recent Israeli military operation—the largest since the second intifada—is part of a search for three settlers who went missing near Hebron, and an intensified PA crackdown on Palestinian protesters has occurred alongside it. There was a shocking episode in Hebron, where a march organized in solidarity with hunger striking prisoners amid the Israeli military incursion ended with Palestinian security forces violently dispersing protesters and arresting journalists. There were also outrageous scenes in Ramallah where angry stone throwers were first attacked by Israeli soldiers and subsequently confronted by the Palestinian police, who shot at them. Such events are not coincidences. Amid numerous similar instances, they show a highly sophisticated security coordination between the two sides.

As a result, social media has been filled with angry comments. One in particular captured my attention: "Palestinian and Israeli securities are changing the working shift." Such irony is painful, but also telling. It also makes clear that there is now a need to put the Palestinian security sector under systematic scrutiny, and reveal its actual function and role.

The Roots of Palestinian Security Reform

In 2003, former Israeli Prime Minister Ariel Sharon delivered a speech before the Herzliya Conference—the most important strategic annual gathering in Israel—in which he demanded that the PA adopt a set of reforms to be implemented in three main phases as a precondition for any future negotiations. Most observers considered the speech's contents Sharon's electoral program. While the demands included financial, institutional, media, and even educational reforms, the priority was a fundamental restructuring of the Palestinian security sector. According to Sharon's perspective, that reform would have three main planks: (1) Dismantling all existing security bodies loyal to Arafat, ones which Sharon described as "terrorists" due to their engagement in armed struggle against Israel during the second intifada; (2) appointing a new minister of interior to oversee the dissolution and outlawing of Palestinian military wings; (3) immediate renewal of Palestinian-Israeli security cooperation. Sharon asserted that "the security reform must accompany a sincere and real effort to stop terrorism, while applying the 'chain of preventive measures' outlined by the Americans: intelligence gathering, arrest, interrogation, prosecution, and punishment."

By the end of the second intifada in 2005, Sharon's vision for Palestinian reform began to emerge, but his illness, long coma, and, later, his death prevented him from celebrating the materialization of his vision.

The PA and Security Reform

Security reform was a top priority in Abbas's electoral agenda, and since he assumed office in 2005, security has been a pillar of his presidency. He wished to transform the Arafatist mode of security—which would sometimes forcefully resist the Israeli military—into strictly inward-oriented security capable of enforcing stability and providing protection to the PA elite. These two objectives were only attainable through effective coordination with Israeli forces.

The reform of the security sector was deep-seated and complex. It covered areas ranging from security doctrine, discipline, training, and equipment to enhanced cooperation with Israel and other regional and international security and intelligence services. For Abbas, the first step was to exclude security personnel deemed to be problematic and unreliable to his project. Thus, he offered them a lucrative retirement deal with a variety of financial advantages and other privileges. Under the banner of "security and order" he moved to disarm the fragmented resistance movement, and also some local gangs that had appeared in the last phase of the intifada. These gangs were mostly composed of former militants who exploited the idea of resistance to run their criminal activity. They were eventually invited to formally join the new PA security force. The PA's overall objective was to maintain a total monopoly over violence and to prevent any potential threat to the newly orchestrated post–Arafat order.

With advice from American and European security consultants, Abbas introduced new regulations to better organize the internal structure of security and to reduce levels of rivalry among the various security branches. In order to ensure loyalty and improve security performance, he initiated a performance-based promotion scheme. Furthermore, in contrast to Arafat's policies, which had deliberately fostered a substantial level of ambiguity in the roles and functions of the multiple security branches that often caused tension among them, Abbas sought to merge security forces into three major categories in accordance with the Roadmap. First, internal, under interior ministry control (civil police, preventive security and civil defense); second, national (national security forces, military intelligence, naval police, military liaison, and presidential security); and third, general intelligence.

When Abbas initiated his security reform agenda in 2005, the Americans and Europeans quickly backed his efforts. The Bush administration initially appointed Lieutenant General William Ward, whose major task, besides overseeing security reform, was to train and prepare security forces to deal with the vacuum left by the Israeli disengagement from the Gaza Strip in 2005. The European Union focused on supervising and training the Palestinian police and justice sector. For this purpose, the European Union established a coordination office in the West Bank, initially called EUCOPPS, and later renamed EUPOL COPPS.

Doctrinal Shift

The striking victory of Hamas in the legislative elections in 2006 led to the halt of international aid to the PA and its security sector. However the Hamas takeover of the Gaza Strip in 2007 sent alarm bells ringing in Tel Aviv, Washington, and other Western capitals, which quickly moved to support the Ramallah-based PA. Security was the most significant destination for Western financial and technical support. This time, however, security reform underwent massive restructuring, especially aimed at reworking the doctrinal foundation of Palestinian security.

Two major factors have played key roles in advancing this shift. The first is linked to the advent of "Fayyadism," referring to the

former PM Salam Fayyad in 2007, whose state-building and neoliberal agenda implied dynamic authoritarianism, and so had a crucial security dimension. Fayyad's security concern was evident in every report published by the subsequent governments, which repeatedly asserted a strong role for security as well as the enforcement of the "rule of law" to create a suitable level of stability to allow private business and investment to flourish. Fayyad's contribution to the security reform has produced a highly privileged sector, consuming over thirty-one percent of the PA annual budget, exceeding other vital sectors such as health, education, and agriculture combined.

> Indeed, for a large segment of the Palestinians, the PA security sector is now viewed as an extension of the occupation. In reaction to PA actions, critics now regularly level charges of treason and betrayal.

In the years 2007 and 2008, Fayyad was behind two campaigns that targeted armed groups and Hamas members in Nablus and Jenin in the northern West Bank. Similar campaigns targeting Jenin were carried out in 2011 and 2012. They were jointly coordinated between the Jenin Governorate and other foreign security in order to "make Jenin a model city for the West Bank."

Such campaigns would have been impossible without the Israeli security establishment's consent and coordination, both of which have quantitatively and qualitatively surpassed the levels of the 1990s. According to an Israeli report, there are now multiple mechanisms for enhanced coordination between the two sides, including a sharp increase in the number of meetings and also regular meetings with senior-level participants. In 2009, coordinated operations numbered 1297, a seventy-two percent increase over 2008, while 2011 witnessed an additional five percent increase compared to 2010.

The second factor is linked with US investment in the PA security establishment, particularly through the engineering of "Dayton's Doctrine." Lieutenant General Keith Dayton, the United States Security Coordinator (USSC) for Israel and the PA who replaced Ward in late 2005, has played a defining role in reshaping the structure and mindset of the PA security forces. His efforts have resulted in the formation of a "new Palestinian man," a professionally trained and disciplined security officer whose function is to blindly follow security orders regardless of the consequences on Palestinians, and to be fully in service to the new US and Israeli security paradigm.

For this purpose, according to the US Government Accountability Office, between 2007 and 2010 the US State Department allocated ninety-nine million dollars to invest in the reconstruction of the PA security infrastructure and capacity-building in the West Bank, and a further 392 million dollars to train and equip security forces. Dayton's mission included recruiting, training, financing, and equipping the PA security forces, including forming the so-called "special battalions" of the National Security Forces (NSF). According to the US State Department, by 2012, the US security mission had trained and equipped nine NSF Special Battalions and two Presidential Guard battalions, totaling over 5500 personnel. These forces have been trained locally and abroad, particularly in Jordan's International Police Training Center. Such trainings are meant to prepare the new forces to carry out internal policing and "counter-terrorism" operations. They offer no defensive skills against external threats and invasions. Security equipment is solely designed for internal suppression and the protection of VIPs, and strategic planning is intended to be in harmony with Israeli military and security objectives.

For Israel and the United States, the PA security reform program is regarded as a success. Israeli President Shimon Peres, in a speech before the European Parliament in 2013, expressed Israel's satisfaction with the state of Palestinian security: "a Palestinian security force was formed. You and the Americans trained it, and now we work together to prevent terror and crime."

PA Elite Protection

When Abbas defended security coordination by calling it a "Palestinian national interest," he was not mistaken—if properly understood from perspective of the PA elite. In this context, the Palestinian national interest should not be understood as the collective interest of the Palestinian people. Indeed, the PA has become a lucrative industry and a comfortable hub for the political-economic elite and the capitalist class and their cronies, increasingly detached from the circumstances of the population which is living under a brutal military-settler regime. The rising class division within Palestinian society has meant that security has had to become a means for the protection of the wealthy and their possessions. Abbas's insistence on preventing any kind of uprising suggests his readiness to use force to suppress protesters, something which has been occurring regularly. Perhaps his major fear stems from the likelihood that any political unrest would ultimately imperil his position, and indeed, on every occasion during which popular demonstrations attempted to approach al-Muqata, his compound in Ramallah, his security forces violently suppressed the demonstrators.

That compound exemplifies the sophistication of PA protection arrangements. Al-Muqata is protected by a professional "Presidential Guard," an elite force of over six thousand men—expanded by the Americans in 2005, before which it had comprised only 2500 men. Recently women fighters have joined the force. The Presidential Guard is structured according to a military-style model, and tasked with safeguarding Abbas and other VIPs, responding to crises, and protecting PA facilities. The Presidential Guard was particularly favored by the US security assistance to strengthen and protect Abbas. It is noteworthy that when the United States halted all forms of aid to Palestinian security after Hamas's victory in the 2006 elections, the Presidential Guard remained the only apparatus to receive direct financial support from the United States. According to Dayton, the United States continued to support this force "because the Presidential Guard reported directly to President Abbas and was not influenced by Hamas, they were considered to be in the game." In fact, in 2006, the Presidential Guard received substantial American aid in the form of equipment, training, and infrastructure worth approximately twenty-six million dollars.

Conclusion

The Palestinian security sector in its current form is far from being part of a national project that would serve the Palestinian cause. Palestinian security forces do not represent the people they are supposed to protect, and their operations and blatant coordination with the Israeli occupation have proven to be destructive to Palestinian national interests. This sector is structured according to predefined Israeli and American plans and conditions. Its functionality and continuity depend on meeting Israeli security concerns and Israeli expectations. Security coordination, in particular, aims to crush any form of resistance, armed or peaceful. The PA elite is highly dependent on security apparatuses to ensure their safety, protect their wealth, and suppress political opposition, even if such opposition were not to pose any direct threat to their rule and privileges.

If there is to be an authentic national security sector, then its forces must be fully restructured in a manner that relates to the real needs and expectations of the people. Above all, Dayton's Doctrine must be completely replaced with values of dignity, self-determination and anti-colonial struggle. This, however, could never happen under the umbrella of Oslo.

A LIFE IN MIDDLE EAST STUDIES

Roger Owen
Foreword by Judith Tucker

Memoir by Roger Owen.
Coming Fall 2016 from Tadween Publishing.

JADMAG PEDAGOGY PUBLICATIONS ISSUE 4.1

Another Palestinian Uprising?

Mouin Rabbani Predictions of a new Palestinian intifada in the Occupied Territories tend to accompany every breakdown in the diplomatic process, announcement of a new colonial expansion project, and Israeli violence against Palestinian life—such as the recent horrific murder of Palestinian infant Ali Dawabsheh by settler terrorists who set fire to his West Bank family home.

Such projections are often prefaced by observations that Palestinians in the Occupied Territories today live under conditions that are, on the whole, considerably worse and more hopeless than those on the eve of either the 1987-1993 or 2000-2004 uprisings.

While it is indeed true that Palestinians, whether within their country or in exile, are currently experiencing unprecedentedly dire circumstances, rebellions are almost never instigated by reality alone. When they are, they tend to take on the character of short-lived and often uncoordinated demonstrations, clashes, and attacks. Indeed, this was the case in the aftermath of the immolation of Jerusalem teenager Muhammad Abu Khdeir by settler terrorists and the pulverization of the Gaza Strip by the Israeli military in the summer of 2014. This is also what will most likely happen in the West Bank this summer: expressions of outrage, a reprisal here and there, and then back to business as usual.

> *An important reason why forecasts about a new insurrection habitually fail to materialize resides in the manner in which the previous two uprisings are remembered and interpreted.*

An important reason why forecasts about a new insurrection habitually fail to materialize resides in the manner in which the previous two uprisings are remembered and interpreted. The conventional history of the 1987 intifada is that a car accident on 8 December at the entrance of the Gaza Strip, in which an Israeli military jeep rammed a Palestinian car and killed four of its occupants, lit a fuse that produced mass demonstrations. The protests first erupted in Gaza's Jabaliya refugee camp and then spread to the Balata refugee camp in the northern West Bank, and quickly engulfed every town, village, and camp throughout the Occupied Territories. Similarly, the 2000 Al-Aqsa Intifada is typically remembered as having been triggered by Ariel Sharon's deliberately provocative incursion into Haram al-Sharif against the backdrop of diplomatic failure at Camp David the preceding month.

While the above renditions provide an accurate description of events, they neglect more important, if largely obscure, dynamics that had been unfolding over the previous years. In the case of the 1987 uprising, the organizations that collectively formed the Palestine Liberation Organization (PLO) had, particularly since their expulsion from Beirut in 1982, conducted intensive organizational work within Palestine and had effectively established an infrastructure of revolt, even if not for the express purpose of unleashing one. The Palestine Communist Party (PCP), Islamic Jihad, and to a lesser extent the Muslim Brotherhood (none of them members of the PLO) had been conducting similar, and in some cases, more intensive grassroots activities.

Secondly, a long-running schism within the PLO was resolved in Algiers in April 1987 with a unity agreement that also for the first time incorporated the PCP into the umbrella organization's ranks. Thus, while it is correct to claim that the subsequent intifada took the PLO—Yasir Arafat and George Habash included—by surprise, the Strike Forces, the Unified National Leadership of the Uprising, and various other committees emerged almost organically on account of previous efforts and developments. For this reason they also had the capacity to expand and sustain the popular rebellion and overcome Israel's increasingly furious attempts to pacify the Occupied Territories.

Although the 2000 uprising was a very different animal, there were important similarities. As in 1987, the spontaneous demonstrations and, in the latter case, initially random armed attacks were quickly channeled into an organizational framework by a leadership keen to use the developments as leverage in its relationship with Israel and the United States. Hence Fatah's newly-formed Al-Aqsa Martyrs' Brigades, which drew upon the movement's organizational infrastructure and Palestinian Authority (PA) security forces, both fostered by Arafat, quickly transformed what were essentially disturbances into an insurgency. It lasted long enough for the Islamist Hamas movement to conclude that it was more than a transient show of force by Arafat and to play an increasingly prominent role in the rebellion itself. The sometimes violent rivalries between the various Palestinian organizations and factions involved in this uprising notwithstanding; after 2000 Arafat never turned his guns primarily against his own people.

The situation today could not be more different than that of 1987 and 2000. To begin with, there is an unprecedentedly deep schism within the Palestinian national movement, and as Palestinian analyst Jamil Hilal has argued, neither the Ramallah nor Gaza authorities will tolerate an uprising against Israel for fear it could be instrumentalized by their Palestinian rivals against themselves. Hilal also argues that Palestinian society has become so fragmented, atomized, and neoliberalized that the prospects for sustained collective action are today not on the cards.

It can in fact be argued that the Palestinian national movement, at least for the present, no longer exists. The PLO exists in name only, while Fatah — traditionally its spinal cord—has been thoroughly decimated during the past decade, primarily by its own leadership rather than by Israel or Hamas. It now hovers between

Jabalia Refugee Camp, Gaza Strip in 1988. Image by Robert Crom via Flickr.

disintegration and extinction. In a society that has traditionally been highly mobilized, the largest constituency today is "none of the above."

Similarly, the regional equation in 2015 is fundamentally different than it was in the late 1980s or the beginning of this millennium. While the Arab world may at these previous junctures have been preoccupied with Iraq and Iran, its governments felt compelled to at least demonstrate solidarity with the Palestinians and advocate on their behalf in international fora. Today, most of these states either do not have functioning governments or are too busy ensuring their own survival.

The situation today could not be more different than that of 1987 and 2000.

In addition, Palestinian diaspora communities had remained relatively coherent and cohesive until recent years. Not only were they able to organize in support of their compatriots in the Occupied Territories, but they also benefited from these uprisings; it is often forgotten that the first significant achievement of the 1987 intifada was to compel Lebanon's Amal movement and its Syrian sponsor to lift the siege of Palestinian refugee camps in Beirut. These communities have since been thoroughly marginalized by the Oslo agreements and a reconfigured Palestinian political system, and in recent years been decimated or shattered in countries like Iraq, Libya, and Syria.

Even if the above mitigating factors were overcome, the present Palestinian leaderships, and particularly that in Ramallah, are averse to popular mobilization. Hamas has essentially committed to conducting only defensive operations except in the most extreme of circumstances, while the PA in Ramallah has been systematically conducting offensive operations for most of the past decade, but against its own people and precisely in order to obstruct the emergence of a serious challenge to Israel's occupation. Indeed, such activities go well beyond the consistent arrests of Hamas and Islamic Jihad operatives, which might be

explained away as an act of PA self-preservation, and include brutal attacks on various forms of peaceful protest, such as those calling for a Palestinian moratorium on negotiations with Israel or denouncing Israel's periodic assaults on the Gaza Strip. This lies at the heart of the increasingly widespread demand for an end to the PA's "security coordination" with Israel. There is good reason that the end of the 2000 intifada is often dated 11 November 2004, the day of Arafat's death.

In conclusion, observations that the Palestinians have not had it so bad since 1948 should reference not only the various indicators that would lead one to suggest another uprising is imminent, but also those factors that together conspire against renewed rebellion. The latter are of course not permanent, but their transformation requires a combination of time, effort, vision, commitment, leadership, and especially hard work. Only then will there be an organizational infrastructure that can once again channel popular fury and mobilize, organize, and sustain a new Palestinian intifada.

[This article was originally published by Middle East Institute. An earlier version of this article was published by Al Jazeera America.]

Jadaliyya جدليّة

www.jadaliyya.com

JADMAG PEDAGOGY PUBLICATIONS ISSUE 4.1

Rebuilding Gaza Needs Freedom and Normality – Not Just Aid

Sara Roy In the near three decades that I have been involved with Gaza and her people, I have never seen the kind of physical and psychological destruction that I see there today.

In all Gaza's long and tormented history, there is no precedent for its extraordinarily dangerous position in 2014. The situation is dangerous not only for Gazans, but for Israelis as well; as the scholar Jean-Pierre Filiu recently wrote: "If there is ever to be Israeli-Palestinian peace–with all other options having been exhausted–Gaza will be the foundation, and the keystone."

This is because Gaza has long been, and remains, the heart of Palestinian nationalism and resistance to Israeli occupation. The war in the summer of 2014 was not about rocket fire, Israeli security, or Hamas: it was about subduing and disabling Gaza, something Israel has consistently been trying to do ever since it occupied the territory together with the West Bank nearly fifty years ago.

Israel's principal strategy has long been to prevent the establishment of a Palestinian state by dividing and separating Palestinians, particularly via the annexation of the West Bank. However complete control over the West Bank – the obvious goal of the settlement enterprise and the separation barrier – cannot be achieved as long as Gaza remains a source of resistance and as long as the possibility of a unified Palestinian state exists (which came a step closer last June with the formal announcement of a Palestinian unity government, the proximate cause of the war on Gaza).

Dynamic of Disintegration

The separation and isolation of Gaza from the West Bank was a goal of the 1993 Oslo process–and had the direct and sustained support of the United States, the European Union, and the Palestinian leadership. It has not only precluded the development of a unified political system but has also eliminated the geographic basis of a Palestinian economy, making the creation of a viable Palestinian state a virtual impossibility.

This is the status quo, institutionalized over the past twenty-one years of "peacemaking," that Israel must preserve, and this is the context in which the large-scale destruction of Gaza's civilian life last summer must be understood.

Ultimately, Operation Protective Edge was designed to set in motion what one of my colleagues recently called a "dynamic of disintegration." That disintegration has taken a number of forms, some of them completely unprecedented.

A whole indigenous economy has been all but destroyed, with extensive damage to civilian infrastructure; Gazan society has been reduced to almost complete aid dependence. It has also been radically economically levelled, with the virtual destruction of its middle class and the emergence of a broad new class of "poor."

Gaza's social fabric has greatly weakened, and is now characterized by a new kind of fragility and disempowerment; entire neighborhoods have been eliminated, and their community life destroyed. Emigration is rising fast, and hope for peace with Israel is being abandoned, to a degree never seen before.

Never mind that Gaza's recent devastation, met largely with laissez-faire silence from Western states, is completely unprecedented; the agreed-upon plan for addressing the situation clearly prioritizes limited short-term gain at the cost of a long-term entrenchment of Israel's destructive blockade.

Getting On With It

Despite the size and urgency of the task at hand, efforts to "reconstruct" or "rebuild" Gaza have long been deeply problematic.

Although billions of dollars have been pledged by donors, reconstruction is always planned or implemented within an unchanged (and unchallenged) political framework of continued Israeli occupation, assault, and blockade. Meanwhile, Gaza's subjection to Israeli military attacks and economic sanction is at best ignored and at worst endorsed by key forces in the West, notably the United States and European Union.

However the current attempt at reconstruction is a new low. Never mind that Gaza's recent devastation, met largely with laissez-faire silence from Western states, is completely unprecedented; the agreed-upon plan for addressing the situation clearly prioritizes limited short-term gain at the cost of a long-term entrenchment of Israel's destructive blockade.

As one donor official put it to me: "If we can get cement and other construction materials into Gaza, it is a win." Another admitted: "Donors backed the plan before they had even seen it."

There are now several published documents describing the reconstruction and recovery plan for Gaza–but the most damning one, the Gaza Reconstruction Mechanism, has not been published (at least to my knowledge), and it is unlikely that it ever will be. Another key document, the Materials Monitoring Unit Project, Project Initiation Document (UNOPS), is available, but has not been widely distributed outside the donor community.

I have seen both documents, the latter in its entirety. They read more like security plans, carefully laying out Israeli concerns and

Marius Arnesen, Housing damaged by Israeli air strikes, Gaza. Image from Wikimedia Commons.

the ways in which the United Nations will accommodate them. They do not speak to the comprehensive recovery of the Gaza Strip.

The reconstruction plan they detail has so many problems that, in my view, it is clearly doomed to fail.

Bad Priorities

The plan calls for a cumbersome administrative and bureaucratic apparatus for project selection and implementation that transfers risk to Palestinian beneficiaries/suppliers and totally ignores the power asymmetries and security realities that will undeniably affect outcomes.

In fact, what is being created is a permanent and complex permit and planning system similar to the one Israel uses in Area C of the West Bank, which is under total Israeli control. This system will be difficult if not impossible to implement, and, as structured, any implementation failure will be blamed on the Palestinians.

Israel will have to approve all projects and their locations and will be able to veto any part of the process on security grounds.

There is no mention of reviving Gaza's export trade or private sector development (other than in relation to specific private-sector companies vetted by the Palestinian Authority and Israel for individually approved projects). Both are essential for rehabilitating Gaza's moribund economy. Similarly, there is no reference to the free movement of people, another urgent need.

No mechanism for accountability or transparency will apply to Israel. Nor will there be any mechanism for resolving disputes, which can only be decided through consensus: the occupier must agree with the occupied.

The plan mainly serves to legitimize Israel's preferred security narrative. According to the UNOPS document, the outcome of the reconstruction project must be:

the establishment of an intermediate system of dual-use items monitoring that will facilitate the import approval of construction materials and machinery into Gaza. This will be achieved

through the reduction of [Israeli] security concerns of materials being diverted for use in the enhancement of military capabilities and terrorist capacities.

Meanwhile, not only will the blockade of Gaza be strengthened, but responsibility for maintaining the blockade is in effect being transferred to the United Nations, which is tasked with monitoring the entire process. As a colleague working as an analyst in Jerusalem so succinctly put it: "Israel retains the power, the United Nations assumes the responsibility and the Palestinians bear the risk."

The document also makes it clear that the donors are the singular funding source for Gaza's reconstruction; Israel assumes no financial responsibility. The UNOPS document has only this to say about the Israeli role: "The [government of Israel] plays no operational role other than approvals and as recipient of the monitoring reports. As such consultation and approval will be required in the development of the report templates."

> *Life in Gaza cannot be rebuilt with cement and cash handouts.*

Assuming, for the sake of argument, that the plan is successfully implemented, its intended outcome is still completely unclear. It does nothing to explain what kind of economy is supposed to be enabled, or what exactly is being rebuilt. Is it what was lost in 2000, 2006, 2007, 2008-09, 2012 or 2014? Is it people's lives and livelihoods?

Beyond Bricks

After all, reconstruction is not simply about buildings and public works: it is about securing a real future, and creating a sense of place, possibility, and security. Life in Gaza cannot be rebuilt with cement and cash handouts.

Of course, people desperately need assistance. What is at issue is the terms on which that assistance will be provided, and what political ends it will serve. Gaza does not just need aid; it needs freedom and the right to interact normally with the world. Anything short of this is unsustainable.

More than twenty years after the so-called peace process began, the donor community funding the rebuilding effort still has big questions to answer. In the absence of a political resolution to the Israeli-Palestinian conflict, it is shocking that the occupation and continued dispossession of more than four million Palestinians in Gaza and the West Bank continues to be tolerated by the West.

Equally, the blockade, the unravelling of Gaza's economy, and the widening impoverishment of 1.75 million people in the Gaza Strip (a great many of them children) are met not with outrage, but with support from Western governments.
The truth is that as long as humanitarian aid is used to address political problems, all "reconstruction" will mean for Gaza is continued ruination.

JADMAG PEDAGOGY PUBLICATIONS ISSUE 4.1

Gaza Reconstruction Mechanism: Profiting Israel, Entrenching the Blockade

Nuriya Oswald

Israel's eight-year, ongoing closure of the Gaza Strip maintains a protracted humanitarian crisis and prevents access to fundamental rights and freedoms for the population of almost two million Palestinians. The International Committee of the Red Cross and the UN Commission of Inquiry on the 2014 Gaza Conflict, have condemned the siege as unlawful collective punishment while the European Union has long considered it an illegal closure. After Israel's July-August 2014 full-scale military assault on Gaza, the United Nations and the international community felt obliged to facilitate reconstruction. They did not, however, feel it necessary to pressure Israel to lift the closure and blockade. This helps to explain support for a futile Gaza Reconstruction Mechanism (GRM) established through the United Nations. Today, not one home that was destroyed in the 2014 bombardment has been rebuilt.

Rather than challenge Israel's siege and systematic attacks, the GRM is entrenching the closure. Moreover, the GRM is financially benefitting Israel. The same politics that have allowed an illegal occupation to endure for decades today undergird a reconstruction mechanism that does not reconstruct the Gaza Strip, but instead consolidates and incentivizes the continued suffering of Palestinians.

In/Efficacy of the Gaza Reconstruction Mechanism

On 7 July 2014, Israel launched a full-scale military offensive it codenamed "Operation Protective Edge" (OPE). The fifty-one-day offensive was comprised of an intense campaign of military attacks by land, air, and sea against the Gaza Strip and resulted in the killing of 2,217 people in Gaza, over seventy percent of whom were civilians: including 556 children, 293 women, and hundreds of elderly and disabled people. According to Al Mezan's documentation, Israeli forces either partially or fully destroyed at least 31,974 housing structures, many of which hosted multiple housing units. Israeli forces destroyed and damaged civilian and public infrastructure en masse, including medical, sanitation, water, education, and electricity facilities.

Rather than challenge Israel's siege and systematic attacks, the GRM is entrenching the closure.

The GRM was set up as a temporary agreement between the Palestinian Authority and the Israeli governments. Brokered by the United Nations in September 2014, the mechanism's primary purpose is to enable re/construction after the 2014 bombardment on Gaza. In light of the long-term closure and siege of Gaza, the stakeholders agreed that the mechanism was "an important step towards the objective of lifting all remaining closures." Notwithstanding these platitudes, the GRM has been counter-productive. Rather than ease and eventually end the siege, the GRM further institutionalizes the closure/blockade by strengthening Israel's mechanisms of control over the Gaza Strip. The United Nations, with Palestinian Authority involvement, oversees the movement of goods, which it tracks and compiles in a database. Israel then reviews this database to determine which construction materials will be permitted entry into Gaza.

> *Without oversight of the manufacturing and purchasing of cement in Israel, Israel cannot be held accountable for inappropriate financial gains for the role it has assumed in the destruction and reconstruction of Gaza.*

This "security" measure, as stated by Israel, is allegedly supposed to ensure that the materials do not end up with Palestinian resistance groups in Gaza who might use the materials in military related activities. However, many people in Gaza who receive materials do not have the funds to cover the manpower necessary for construction. Rather than use them for their stated purpose, they then proceed to sell part or all of their cement on the black market. The sale of the cement on the black market is not monitored, and materials can easily be sold to individuals connected to armed resistance groups. Israel's agreed GRM is therefore not addressing the security concerns it states because once the cement is delivered to the recipient in Gaza, there is no controlling where it goes. Israel's oversight function is much more about control than it is about security, and it is facilitated by the GRM.

The GRM has not been effective in reconstruction and/or construction. Of the 8,377 houses that Israel fully destroyed, not a single one has been rebuilt. Of the 23,597 houses that were partially destroyed, only approximately five percent have been rebuilt. At present, approximately twelve thousand people are still living in temporary shelters throughout Gaza. According to Oxfam International, at the current rate of reconstruction and without lifting the closure/blockade, it could take more than one-hundred years to rebuild Gaza's "housing, education, and health infrastructure."

The international community has also failed to make due on their pledges from the Cairo Conference on Palestine where several states pledged 5.4 billion US dollars to Palestine, with approximately half of the funds earmarked for the reconstruction of Gaza. Almost two-thirds of these funds have not been delivered to Gaza.

Gaza after bombing by Israeli Defense Forces, 2014. Image by Muhammad Sabah/ via B'Tselem and Wikimedia Commons.

The international community's approach has been to wait out one futile peace process after another for decades. The issues faced by Palestinians with the GRM in Gaza are exemplary of the international community's overall approach to Palestine: to support flawed, flimsy mechanisms subject to Israel's ultimate discretion. The international community accepts them as a temporary measure that appears "better than nothing," so to speak. Here, the international community seems to overlook two fundamental flaws. First, the GRM causes further immediate and long-term harm in Gaza. As such it is not a temporary measure. Secondly, the GRM provides a strengthened framework through which the occupiers of Gaza can maintain the closure and blockade with greater ease.

We are discussing the occupation of Palestine today because of the Oslo Accords that were recklessly instituted by Israel, the Palestinian Liberation Organization, and the international community as a first step towards self-determination. Now, two decades since the accords, Palestinians live under the same framework of occupation and are further than ever from achieving peace. Aside from acceding to the Rome Statute–carried out under heavy pressure from the Palestinian population–the Palestinian Authority has by and large responded cosmetically to Israel's escalating aggression and remained seemingly unmoved by shifting political winds. Conversely, the Israeli government has become increasingly bold and transparent in carrying out measures to further distance the two parties from peace. Nowhere can we see this more clearly than in the surprisingly transparent speeches by Prime Minister Benjamin Netanyahu in his election speeches advocating for more settlements and promising that there will be no Palestinian state.

The international community must fulfill its obligations to the Palestinian people according to international law. The closure of Gaza must be fully and unconditionally lifted. This requires applying political pressure on Israel. Any mechanism operating within the illegal framework of the occupation and complicit with the occupation authorities is not only insufficient as a temporary measure, but it also actually entrenches the infringement on the rights and freedoms of the Palestinian population.

In the aftermath of a devastating military campaign of the Gaza Strip in 2014, lifting the closure is imperative. The GRM is not the answer. Nor can it be. There is no need for bureaucratic, dysfunctional mechanisms that foil critical reconstruction efforts. Nor is there room for mechanisms that institutionalize unlawful policies as the GRM entrenches the policies of closure and blockade. There is a need to lift the closure now and allow people to build their homes and their lives; to allow them access to justice and dignity.

Who Profits? And Accountability

The lack of clarity as to the functioning and responsibility of each stage of the GRM means that not only could the Israeli government be making huge financial gains through the mechanism, but it could also be purchasing cement for Gaza reconstruction from illegal settlements in the West Bank. The GRM does not contain an oversight mechanism of Israel. Without oversight of the manufacturing and purchasing of cement in Israel, Israel cannot be held accountable for inappropriate financial gains for the role it has assumed in the destruction and reconstruction of Gaza.

In the aftermath of a devastating military campaign of the Gaza Strip in 2014, lifting the closure is imperative. The GRM is not the answer.

As the occupying power engaged in combat action, which harms civilians and destroys civilian infrastructure in violation of the laws of war, Israel has the responsibility to assume the role and absorb the costs of reconstruction. Instead, it is now in a position where it directly profits from the limited reconstruction it permits. Additionally, Israel has designed an infallible system of impunity within its domestic judicial system to block justice and shield government decision makers and military leaders from being held to account for violations stemming from the policies of the occupation, including the full-scale military bombardments of Gaza. This reality, implicitly and explicitly supported by the members of the international community that have hindered Palestinian access to justice and accountability at the United Nations as well as the International Criminal Court, has made the occupation a lucrative project. Far from deterring further harm, this arrangement has encouraged the devastating cycle of violence repeatedly wrought on Gaza.

JADMAG PEDAGOGY PUBLICATIONS ISSUE 4.1

The Limits of Humanitarianism

Max Ajl

The prose of collapse increasingly punctuates reports and communiques concerned with the well-being of the Palestinians in the Gaza Strip. As early as 2006, as the Israeli siege slowly settled into place, reports cautioned of the collapse of the health system. On 4 January 2009, the Israeli human rights organization Gisha warned, "Gaza's water and sewage system is on the verge of collapse following bombardments that have destroyed electricity lines." On 27 May 2009, the European Commission announced, "The banking system in Gaza is on the verge of collapse because there is not enough physical cash... Our projects cannot receive the necessary cash." On 3 September 2014, the United Nations observed, "Even before the latest crisis in the Gaza Strip, the tiny enclave's local economy was in a state of total collapse." And on 21 May 2015, the World Bank released a report with the headline, "Gaza Economy on the Verge of Collapse."

As the weight of cumulative bombardments grows heavier, the solvent of Israeli siege accelerates the Gaza Strip's infrastructure's disintegration. It began with the gossamer structures of public health, and moved on to the tougher but vulnerable water and sewage systems, the basic infrastructure of urban civilization for millennia. As the siege advanced and grew more sophisticated, Israeli regulations targeted the banking system and prevented the flows of hard currency that are its lifeblood. In the last years, it has been the "collapse" of the economy.

I examine here the notion of "collapse" through a historical analysis of the escalating attack on the Gaza Strip since 2006, as well as a critical reading of the latest World Bank report. Increasingly, international and local institutions have used the idea of collapse to remove Israeli policies from a larger settler-colonial framework, one linked to the foreign policies of the Western powers. Their containment project has absorbed these proliferating notions of collapse. Such concepts are intimately linked to a humanitarian discourse which denies political claims, and an economic history which conceals the dynamic interaction between Israeli accumulation and Palestinian destitution. Finally, I suggest that it is only when the institutions discuss solutions, or even political negotiators, that the veil slips, and the core colonial prerogative, the right to decide who can speak for the colonized, flashes into view.

Collapse or Colonial Containment?

Collapse is both analogy and policy. As analogy, it is a way of raising the volume. It is the sound of the international institutions' agitating at their maneuvering limits. Any conversation with the staff of international NGOs in the Gaza Strip reveals considerable sympathy for the Palestinians of the Gaza Strip, if not the cause in general, along with sharp antipathy to the Israeli regime. But their mandate does not extend to dealing with the root cause of the siege. As the World Bank admits, Israel "tightened movement of goods and people in and out of Gaza in 2006 following the January 2006 victory of Hamas and the formation of the Hamas-led PA government in March 2006." As it goes on to warn, "A status quo in Gaza is unsustainable and could have further incalculable socioeconomic and ultimately human consequences." Nevertheless, such institutions are not–directly–political actors. Their task, or their capabilities, is at best to keep the situation frozen in time, to prevent "collapse," and to keep the Palestinians of the Strip alive. But not much more. And so the desperate rhetoric of collapse can also be a paralyzing agent, meant to produce passivity on the readers' part.

Increasingly, international and local institutions have used the idea of collapse to remove Israeli policies from a larger settler-colonial framework, one linked to the foreign policies of the Western powers.

Oddly, the Israeli government itself is also keen to prevent collapse. As *Wikileaks* cables have demonstrated, "Israeli officials have confirmed to [US] Embassy officials on multiple occasions that they intend to keep the Gazan economy functioning at the lowest level possible consistent with avoiding a humanitarian cdisrisis." Indeed, "Israeli officials have confirmed...on multiple occasions that they intend to keep the Gazan economy on the brink of collapse without quite pushing it over the edge." This is a process through which, in the words of Sherene Seikaly discussing British colonial policy in Palestine, "The provision of welfare [becomes] inextricable from political containment."

Such violent freezes, represented with words like stasis, verge, and brink, are long-standing Israeli tools. It has increasingly resorted to them as the older kind of colonial domination, mass expulsion, became impractical. In its place, Israel implements fixes intended to conceal and consolidate the colonial process, while also managing and containing resistance to it. One such fix was the "peace process," a partial response to the first intifada. Another was the Israeli disengagement from the Strip, designed to place the peace process in "formaldehyde," in the words of Dov Weisglass, then the senior adviser to Ariel Sharon. The aim was to keep Palestinians and especially the Palestinians in the Gaza Strip–those, in the words of Darwish, "most capable, among us, of dis¬turb¬ing the enemy's mood and his comfort"–locked in colonial control's historical, political, and geographical limits. As those limits tighten, nested in one another like Russian dolls, the project advances.

Indeed, each effort at political containment reflects an advance of the colonial project, visible as if through a glass, darkly. For with each one, the situation in the Strip worsens. The World Bank report warning of "collapse" hides the nature of the US-Israeli

Watchtower, Rafah, Gaza Strip border with Egypt, April 2009. Image by Marius Arnesen via Wikimedia Commons.

project, even as its prescription to avert such a fall follows imperial surrender terms to the letter.

Collapse and the Denial of Politics

Equally insidious is the entire technocratic-developmentalist framework. This framework does not fragment politics; it denies it altogether. A brief glimpse at the "economy" the World Bank crafts and its construction methods reveals the prior colonial epistemology.

This epistemology is evident in the quantitative material that the World Bank mobilizes to craft the Gaza Strip's economy. The report speaks of "an analysis of Gaza's stark economic decline over the past twenty years and its human impact. It also presents a mix of policies that should ensure sustainable development of the Gaza strip and put an end to human suffering therein." The report goes on to note that "Real per capita income is thirty-one percent lower in Gaza than it was twenty years ago," and that "Its manufacturing sector—once significant—has shrunk by as much as sixty percent in real terms," far more per-capita. Industry is now at some five percent as industrial establishments are starved of traded inputs, their export channels blocked. Indeed, Israel has simply destroyed many of them.

The starting point for this analysis is the 1993 Oslo Accords. But why start there? Why not start in 1967, as the occupation began to prevent any possibility of industrial development? Why not start in 1948, when Israeli colonialism created the Strip as a political-geographical unit? Why not start in 1917 as the Strip came

under British mandatory rule, devoted more to minimalist welfare than any meaningful development? Indeed, to speak at all of the "Gazan economy" is a novelty, and to set 1993 as an economic baseline is a political choice. It reinforces the Israeli project of fragmenting the Palestinian people, turning them into Gazans, West Bankers, 1948 Palestinians or "Israeli Arabs," and various diaspora communities. The discursive fragmentation is a mirror of a fragmented politics and people. This discourse is also a way, as with all colonial projects, to violently deny history. Gaza City's history is that of a trading entrepôt, at the crossroads of three continents. It used to be a port-city on par with Haifa. Gaza City is Gaza City as it is and not as it could have been because of Israeli violence. The colonial denial of history is most visible in the absurd comment of 2010 that "Gaza was a golden opportunity tragically missed. Instead of building a Mediterranean Dubai, Hamas diverted every resource to enslaving its people while attacking" Israelis. But this present always-already "collapse" is not due to a twenty-year occupation but well over a century of what Riyad Mousa calls "settler capitalist" predation. Three empires, the British, French, and US, have underwritten and benefited from this predation.

The report notes that it is flows of goods and money that are increasingly constricted, with the majority of the tunnels destroyed, hammering its "constrained economy." During the war itself:

> 963 enterprises in the manufacturing sector were hit during the war reducing its output by twenty-eight percent in 2014 compared to the previous year. Agriculture also suffered as a large part of Gaza's farms and arable

land were ruined by military activity or eaten up by the enlarged security buffer zone that was established near the border during the war, and hence its 2014 output declined by thirty-one percent.

Youth unemployment consequently reached over sixty percent. The part of the population that is aid-dependent reached eighty percent, and the percentage of poor reached thirty-nine percent. Electricity supply only meets forty-six percent of needs, while water quality remains poor, and there is a lack of access to sanitation services. Even in 2008, the aquifer was overdrawn by two hundred per cent, accelerating the infusion of seawater and making the water supply unfit for human consumption. Sewage is pumped untreated into the Mediterranean, where some of it percolates back into the aquifers. As a result, water-borne illness is rising.

> *The blockade becomes a disease, which causes certain "symptoms," like ongoing de-development. A stronger and healthier economy might do well without "life support," in other words, donor aid. But donor aid is not "life support." It comes with conditions.*

As the report goes on to note, "donor aid and remittances have been the most significant drivers of Gaza's economy," and although the degree of dependence is not clear, "it is certain that aid and remittances are almost the only source of foreign exchange inflows that fuels consumption in Gaza—which stands at 118 percent of its depressed GDP." Aid comes from the United Nations Relief and Workers Agency (UNRWA), non-PA donor projects, and the PA. The PA spends about 1.6 billion US dollars a year in the Strip. That is fifty-eight percent of its revenue, while it only collects about thirteen percent of its revenues there.

The report then notes that in 2014 PA and UNRWA expenditures came to 1.8 billion US dollars, fifty-eight percent of the Gaza Strip's estimated GDP, while World Bank staff estimate that remittances, some other donor projects, and flows to the Hamas government came to another nine hundred million US dollars, totaling roughly ninety percent of the Strip's GDP. Much of PA spending is on staff salaries and social assistance benefits. The report does not note that, as in the West Bank, Palestinians in the Gaza Strip on the PA payroll are perhaps less likely to move sharply against it as the occupation's subcontractor. It is by design that the needs of the Palestinians in the Strip are dependent on capital flows intended for a specific purpose. Even UNRWA is now facing a Western-imposed "austerity budget" whose only plausible goal can be to break the political will of the Palestinian people through collective punishment. Moreover, the inability to accumulate capital locally, the reliance on external flows, is not novel. It has been a structural feature of the Gaza Strip since at least 1967, when Israel turned the Strip into an appendage to its own accumulation process.

The Colonialism of the World Bank

The World Bank's analysis sidesteps the colonial genealogy of the siege. It quietly admits that Israel imposed the blockade in response to the Hamas victory in the 2006 elections. The report also concedes the origins of the premeditated ruin of field and factory in the Gaza Strip in "war and the blockade." But it then implies that the siege was a response to subsequent "violence" and genuine security concerns, as opposed to Israel's inability to deal with the Hamas movement's "peace offensive"–its refusal to compromise on minimal Palestinian national demands. Since the World Bank misdiagnoses the problem, it is predictable that its prescriptions are removed from any meaningful reference points: "The potential shown above and quick rebounds of Gaza's economy that followed cycles of violence when conditions improved provide sufficient comfort that Gaza's economy can be removed from life support quickly if the blockade is lifted and the right economic and governance policies are put in place." Here the vital metaphors re-emerge, but the economy ceases being an ecological system. It becomes something like a hospital patient. The blockade becomes a disease, which causes certain "symptoms," like ongoing de-development. A stronger and healthier economy might do well without "life support," in other words, donor aid. But donor aid is not "life support." It comes with conditions. USAID's notorious demand for their grantees to disassociate from the parties supporting the liberation project, known colloquially in Washington, DC as "terrorist groups," is one example.

"Governance" is, of course, the antiseptic lie under which the World Bank constantly smuggles entire suites of undemocratic directives. As it notes, what is needed is "institutional strengthening under PA's leadership...Building legitimate institutions in Gaza that enjoy the support of the international community." It "requires a unified Palestinian government in both West Bank and Gaza that can be a partner to multilateral and bilateral donors and substantial donor support to rebuild Gaza's infrastructure and homes, and it requires the lifting of the blockade." Then, "Once the Palestinian Authority is fully in charge of Gaza's public sector, it will have to take prompt actions to ensure sustainability of its governance arrangements in Gaza" through tax arrangements, and only then will Israel lift the blockade. But such "solutions" are historical, too, the outcome of setbacks in the struggle for self-determination. It is "improved governance," not liberation, which is the goal. But who made such a determination, and why? When did the "international community" become the reference point?

Meanwhile, the World Bank only goes so far as to distantly rue the events in the run-up to the war, noting "that the effort to create these institutions with the appointment of the consensus government in 2014 has not made much progress." What such oblique formulations sidestep is that it is Hamas's refusal to surrender which led to the massacre which disrupted the "progress" of a unity government in 2014. The emphasis on the PA, the darling of those governments, is not a surprise. Indeed, it is a violation of US law for anyone to support the "public sector" in the Gaza Strip, which Hamas governs. It is in this manner that the World Bank follows colonial orders, accepting only "legitimate" or legitimized interlocutors from the colonized society.

What makes them legitimate is that they no longer hold up the national banner.

In the tightly engineered pressure and torture chamber that is the Gaza Strip, no sudden collapse seems to occur. Flows are cut, infrastructure is destroyed, lives ended, children traumatized, hopes snapped, futures denied, generations lost. No GDP indicator can tell us when an economy has collapsed or if it is merely on the verge.

The Ends of Collapse

This tableau, which resembles a hostage negotiation, is the "collapse" that the World Bank authorities perpetually peer on to, as they peek over the precipice, in the Strip. The use of the word in relation to that other nebulous creation of early twentieth century political economy, "the economy," here is both curious and instructive. Such rhetoric summons the economy as an architecture, a physical system, an organic entity, which without the prescribed life support will collapse.

But in the tightly engineered pressure and torture chamber that is the Gaza Strip, no sudden collapse seems to occur. Flows are cut, infrastructure is destroyed, lives ended, children traumatized, hopes snapped, futures denied, generations lost. No GDP indicator can tell us when an economy has collapsed or if it is merely on the verge. The World Bank admits as much, noting, "numbers…fail to portray the degree of suffering of Gaza's citizens due to poor electricity and water/sewerage availability, war-related psychological trauma, limited movement, and other adverse effects of wars and the blockade." Indeed, "collapse" works much as notions of "crisis" in so-called advanced capitalist economies. It is a way of avoiding the reality that crises are not of the system, but in the system. They always benefit some and hurt others. "Collapse" sidesteps that it is Israeli colonial capitalism above all that stunts the Strip.

If "collapse" means civilizations cascading to a lesser social complexity, what could collapse mean in the context of the Gaza Strip? What is happening is so much crueler. For it is deliberately inflicted. First Israel concentrates of people into an impossibly packed coastal salient. Then it builds walls and strings barbed wire around it. Then, when the trapped people resist, Israel uses the very modern tools, copying US sanctions policy in Iraq, of cutting off the Strip's infrastructure from the world.

There is No Collapse. There is Demolition.

What the World Bank's rhetoric helps hide is that near-collapse has been conscious policy. The recurrence of the word "collapse" is not an accident, not a literary quirk or tic. The brutal suspension of near-collapse is the result of economic and social sabotage. It intends to keep the population of the Gaza Strip in a state of chaos and enfeeblement. But intentions do not always translate into facts on the ground. Despite over a century of relentless efforts, despite the current advance of the Israeli-US-Saudi regional project, Israeli means still have

not matched Israeli ends: a terminal defeat of Palestinian nationalism.

As such we must criticize the World Bank reports, their narratives, their gaps, and their prescriptions. For the World Bank's reactiveness is a product of colonialism–but also helps reinforce it. Because colonialism, like any relationship of oppression, seeks to normalize itself. It has an amnesiac quality. It seeks to present the present as without history. As a result, we swim in a sea of technical problems awaiting quick "fixes," political crises awaiting "governance" reforms.

But ultimately, the World Bank's governance-oriented framework quietly demands that the Palestinian movement surrender. It does so in part, as I have argued, by starting Palestinian economic history with Oslo. The settler-colonial framework has suggested one resolution: that history matters. And not just that it matters in general. But that a much longer arc of history matters, and that it sets the limits within which any political project, whether in Palestine or elsewhere, may proceed. Lately, many use that framework to suggest a quick fix–decolonize!–or reduce it to sentiment. Neither perspective helps in seeing history as having brought all of us to where we are. Over a century of Palestinian and broader Arab resistance to Zionism, with all of that resistance's lights and shadows, has molded the shape of Zionism in important ways, sometimes opening important spaces and fissures in the Zionist project. Furthermore, any intervention in historical processes starts from existing strengths. In this case, those are the resistance movements as they actually exist in Palestine and in the region. Settler-colonialism, as a story that begins with imperialism and a settlement movement, is a story we tell about Israel–one we tell for a purpose. Or perhaps there are many purposes vying with one another, with the stories varying alongside the purposes. But none of the histories we tell are politically innocent.

> *But ultimately, the World Bank's governance-oriented framework quietly demands that the Palestinian movement surrender.*

Once committed to telling a tale of continuous colonial settlement, we ought to understand that it should mean telling another story, too: of the force, in the words of Darwish, which will in Gaza "continue to explode," as "it wants to expel the enemy out of its clothes." It is "Gaza's way of declaring that it deserves to live." If settler colonialism becomes a purely academic analysis, a history which excludes the story of the resistance, which is not only the current project of defying Zionism but also has constituted the underside of settler-colonialism, then it becomes a very problematic history indeed.

JADMAG PEDAGOGY PUBLICATIONS ISSUE 4.1

Planning Under Occupation: Elastic Geographies and 'Area C'

Lamya Hussain

In recent years there has been growing concern about Israel's planning regime and its operations across the West Bank. In particular, organizations have expressed their apprehension toward the growing number of demolitions, eviction orders, and restrictions in Area C. According to the 1995 Oslo Accords, Area C of the occupied Palestinian territories (oPt) amounts to an estimated sixty-two percent of the West Bank. It is rich in land and water, and critical to the sustainable long-term development of a future viable Palestinian state. Israeli restrictions on planning and development in Area C have created systemic poverty and instability across local Palestinian communities, undermining developmental possibilities. Additionally, Israel has tightened its military control of Area C of late, and increased restrictions on the delivery of international aid and humanitarian assistance. This process has produced new threats for an already vulnerable population, and brings into question both the legitimacy and responsibility of Israel as an occupying power.

Since 2005, the Israeli Civil Administration (ICA) has initiated a number of "special outline plans" for Palestinian villages in Area C. These plans carve out territorial arrangements, which set in motion a series of home demolitions and other civil-military orders that forcibly displace the local population. These conditions are designed in order to maintain Israeli hegemony in Area C. Planning tools play a critical role in how those on the ground make and implement those decisions. In response to the slowly deteriorating status of Area C communities, the Office of the Quartet Representative initiated planning activities in 2008 for at least fourteen Palestinian villages there. The ICA adopted the new initiative, but appointed itself as the governing body, which will approve or disapprove any plans submitted on behalf of the Palestinians in Area C.

The result is that the Israeli planning regime disadvantages the Palestinians in Area C on two levels. First, it creates systematic barriers to development. Second, it creates an institutional reality, which would oversee, and in a sense implement, Palestinian planning according to its own interests and master-plans. Indeed, in spite of that 2008 directive, by 2009 demolition of Palestinian structures, homes, and property reached alarming levels. Local and international human rights organizations sharply criticized this trend. The rising attention to the status of Area C led UN Office for the Coordination of Humanitarian Affairs (OCHA) to produce an Area C Humanitarian Response Plan. The UN Humanitarian Country Team (UN HCT) later adopted it. To date, Israel itself has failed to adopt or. As a result, humanitarian actors face real challenges as they attempt to deliver aid and assistance across Area C.

By 2011, frustrations around the restrictions the ICA imposed led stakeholders to consider other avenues to bypass the Israeli planning regime and its Area C practices. The systematic forced displacement of the local population has raised concerns from both local and international stakeholders who view Israeli occupation policy and practice to be in direct violation of both international law and previous agreements. Indeed, between 2010 and 2011, there was a forty percent increase in demolitions of Palestinian structures, property, and homes. These conditions led human rights organizations to demand the transfer of planning powers back to the Palestinian local and district planning committees in order to protect existing structures and to encourage sustainable development for future infrastructure.

The Israeli public relations machine portrays the ICA as a separate administrative and legal body, distinct from the armed forces. However it is really an extended arm of the Israeli military occupation and works parallel to the military in order to maintain and expand its power over the Palestinian territories. The two bodies are joined in a manner which supports a clear Zionist vision toward territory in the West Bank, particularly the natural resource-rich Jordan Valley. By producing legal and administrative deadlocks, the ICA has several tools to shape a complex system, operating through a dizzying array of permits, demolition orders, military zones, and guidelines, all designed to displace and devastate Palestinians' capacities to achieve sustainable livelihoods.

> *The Israeli planning regime disadvantages the Palestinians in Area C on two levels. First, it creates systematic barriers to development. Second, it creates an institutional reality, which would oversee, and in a sense implement, Palestinian planning according to its own interests and master-plans.*

Since the occupation of the West Bank began in 1967, the Jordan Valley in particular has witnessed a heightened military and security presence, which has had a significant impact on the local population. An estimated three-hundred thousand Palestinians lived in the Jordan Valley before the 1967 war. Today, after forty years of occupation, the population in the area has been reduced to perhaps fifty-six thousand. In addition to displacing the local communities, forced urbanization has shifted the livelihoods of local communities from rural to urban. Seventy percent of the residents are concentrated in the city center of Jericho, particularly in parts that are either Area A or B, in order to avert confrontations with either Israeli settlers or the military. Communities that were formerly dependent on farming, livestock, and other rural activities for income have been dramatically reduced–to forty percent of the remaining population.

Agriculture used to be a primary source of livelihood. It has suffered drastically amidst Israeli restrictions on access to resources, development, and infrastructure. A 1968 census documented that, at the time, at least forty-two percent of the Palestinian labor force worked in agriculture.[1] By 2011, this was reduced to about fourteen percent.[2] From 1984 to 2010, the total land dedicated to agriculture decreased from 1,700,000 dunams to 1,105,000 dunams. At least one third of the local arable land is no longer accessible to Palestinians. Furthermore, in 2012 the ICA issued permits to destroy the agricultural networks and structures of at least 242 families in the West Bank. The ICA has particularly targeted the Jordan Valley. The authority has issued several restrictive measures to annex around sixty thousand dunams of Palestinian agricultural lands.[3] This loss of land means that over ninety percent of the remaining Palestinian farming communities in the Jordan Valley have great difficulty cultivating their land amidst the ICA planning regime and restrictions.

On the other hand, Israeli military and planning practices have incubated and strengthened illegal Israeli settlements and their agricultural businesses. An estimated ninety percent of the Jordan Valley is designated as Area C–full Israeli military and civil control. Out of that ninety percent, at least fifty percent is split between military zones, natural reserves, and illegal settlements. This leaves about six percent of the land to the Palestinian population, which has almost no participation and control over their land, mobility, and resources. These conditions have fast-tracked the growth of the Israeli agriculture sector, as illegal settlements and associated businesses are flourishing on Palestinian resources. By taking advantage of the climate, water, and soil conditions, Israeli agribusinesses are able to experiment with crop diversity and produce a variety of goods for export. Furthermore, by monopolizing the production of seeds, Israel also prevents Palestinian farmers and their enterprises from advancing local capacity in agricultural research and development.

Master-Planning: Israeli and Donor-Funded Plans

One key way the Israeli planning regime administers the building and development of Israeli settlement infrastructure is by using "master-plans," a tool of urban planning which factors in the necessary infrastructure for local communities including water, power, sewage, and other necessary human needs. Master planning also involves accounting for the natural growth of the local community, and includes protective measures toward nature reserves and water networks.

There are two sets of policies that are enforced with respect to Palestinians and Israelis in the West Bank. While Israeli settlements, industries, and businesses enjoy support, funds, and social services from the state, Palestinians under Israeli occupation are stripped of their most basic and human rights. The conditions in Area C are exceptionally difficult, as the local Palestinian population is under the complete military and administrative control of the Israeli occupation. The ICA prohibits Palestinian development in Area C under various pretexts, including claiming that the lands are state owned, military firing zones, nature reserves or parks, or are a security area due to their proximity to the Green Line or wall. In the remaining parts

of Area C, the ICA has to preapprove any construction. This applies to all private development, including residences, agricultural structures, or other infrastructure that would help improve the living conditions of the local Palestinian population. A 2011 B'Tselem report notes that the ICA has not approved any master plans for the majority of villages located in Area C. Only sixteen communities have Israeli-approved master-plans. Communities that do not have plans are extremely vulnerable to forced displacement. Communities with existing plans are at constant risk of losing large plots of land and access to resources, and can be easily isolated and disconnected from other parts of the West Bank.

While Israeli settlements, industries, and businesses enjoy support, funds, and social services from the state, Palestinians under Israeli occupation are stripped of their most basic and human rights. The conditions in Area C are exceptionally difficult, as the local Palestinian population is under the complete military and administrative control of the Israeli occupation.

In response to the current ICA-established planning system, the international donor community and other third-party stakeholders have recently heightened efforts to create a parallel planning mechanism. That alternative scheme could include Palestinians in key decision-making processes which affect their communities. By doing so, a parallel planning regime is taking form, which includes donors and their implementing partners–the United Nations and other contractors–the community in question, and representatives from the Palestinian Authority (PA). Each plan is drafted with input from the local community, and is then measured against Israeli master-plans for the area. Furthermore, donor-funded plans are still subject to ICA approval. Ultimately, Israel still enforces its planning restrictions.

For that reason, key civil society agents and human rights groups view donor-led planning with great suspicion. Some claim it to be a direct violation of humanitarian law and the principles as stipulated under UN Security Council Resolution 242, which clearly states that Israel must withdraw all armed forces from the occupied territories of 1967. Critics of donor-led planning also claim that it participates and coordinates with the ICA, and therefore indirectly legitimizes the occupation and its practices in Area C. Still others argue that Israel must be held accountable toward its responsibilities as an occupying power as specified under the Geneva conventions.

Nonetheless, there are few avenues by which the situation on the ground can be quickly and drastically altered. So in the meantime, spectators and stakeholders argue that there is a need to continue investing in humanitarian aid to respond to Palestinian needs. One approach that donors, international organizations, and UN agencies propose is to engage in their own "master-planning" initiatives in order to document and design plans to reflect the needs identified by local Palestinians with respect to individual communities. However, there are critical challenges posed for policymakers, practitioners, and planners who engage in master-planning across the Palestinian territories–particularly in Area C. The main challenge is that the ICA must approve all master-plans, which means that the passing of a sustainable plan for a Palestinian community rests in the hands of those least likely to approve it. This wastes efforts, while the broader process of master-planning leads ceaselessly to the shaping of smaller and broken communities.

Displacement by Design

The core feature of the Israeli occupation can be summarized as *displacement by design*, a process which encompasses designing and shaping the evolving state of Israel, alongside the systematic and continuous displacement of the indigenous population. To do so, Israel employs a variety of means including, war, geog raphy, and law. The combination of tools helps separate Israelis from Palestinians and Palestinians from other Palestinians, in order to formalize Israeli colonial control and structural divisions.

> *The core feature of the Israeli occupation can be summarized as displacement by design, a process which encompasses designing and shaping the evolving state of Israel, alongside the systematic and continuous displacement of the indigenous population.*

In using urban planning to design and organize communities, residences, infrastructures, and resources, Israel is clear in its aim to monopolize resources while annexing Palestinian lands to build Israeli settlements. The Israeli occupation employs planning as a tool to cause shifts in the local geography and territory, thereby serving broader state interests. By using arguments based on planning, the ICA issued roughly 9682 demolition orders between 2000 and 2012 for Palestinian structures. To date, at least 2829 of those structures have been demolished. Between 2006 and 2013, the ICA ordered the demolition of at least 624 Palestinian homes in the West Bank–not including East Jerusalem–which resulted in the displacement of 3075 persons, at least 1457 of them minors.

In 2009 the United Nations reported the highest number of home demolitions in Area C communities, where at least seventy-nine percent of the Palestinians displaced during this period were previously residing in the Jordan Valley. Often times this is done by declaring the area in question as a closed military zone, as in the case of al-Hadidiya village in 2009 where 162 residents were displaced over a short period.[4] This had a critical impact on a relatively small herding community, leaving the remaining families vulnerable to encroaching settlements and military raids.

Other methods to displace communities include designing a web-of-sorts, one that restricts Palestinian access and mobility. There are at least three main checkpoints that limit access into, and movement within, the Jordan Valley. These checkpoints separate people from land and land from the livelihoods of rural communities. In addition to physical barriers designed to restrict, limit, and prevent access to Palestinians, Israel enforces a permit and ID system in order to control individual access. It is evident that both physical and other legal means work toward limiting access to Palestinians, which makes ordinary and daily tasks substantially more difficult. An OCHA report explains how the ICA enforces the planning and permit system:

In order to obtain a building permit, a proposed construction must be consistent with an approved planning scheme–regional, outline, or detailed. In practice, however, the Israeli authorities generally allow Palestinian construction only within the boundaries of an ICA detailed, or special plan, and those plans cover less than one percent of Area C, much of which is already built-up … in the current system applied by the ICA, Palestinians have no role in zoning of Area C land. In addition, they have no input into the development of plans for their communities or in approving construction; Israeli modifications to the Jordanian planning law in force at the start of the occupation eliminated Palestinian community participation and centralized authority for these tasks within the ICA.

Normalizing the Israeli Planning Regime: Donors, PA, and Local Contractors

Recently, donors have emphasized the emerging development and infrastructural needs of Palestinians living in Area C. In addition to basic human needs, the European Union and the World Bank have estimated the monetary importance of Area C and its resources, and their potential impact on the local Palestinian economy–about 3.4 billion dollars. This attracts the interest of the Palestinian private sector, the PA, and other stakeholders, all of whom see a potential in investment and cooperation to access, control, and build on Area C resources.

At the humanitarian level, donors are interested in designing and planning infrastructural projects to meet local community needs. Nonetheless, any structural planning or implementation in Area C requires an approval from the ICA. Therefore, donors and humanitarian organizations continue to struggle with finding a median between funding or implementing critical development projects in Area C or jeopardizing their relationship with the Israeli authorities on whom they are completely dependent operationally.

This raises a series of ethical and legal questions for third-party stakeholders operating in the Palestinian territories. What, exactly, is the role of humanitarian agents in an ongoing conflict zone where land relations are at the core of the dispute? How can the international assistance program assist the needs of Palestinians in Area C without negotiating their historical right to the land through direct coordination with the ICA and its policies? By gaining approval on all plans that detail building permits, and allocate key resources, is the international community and its efforts merely mediating occupation policy between the Israelis and Palestinians?

In recent years, third-party stakeholders have revised the term "master planning" in an attempt to create a parallel approach to the Israeli planning regime as a proposed solution to the development-based needs of Palestinians. The Office of the Quartet Representative website proudly announces that around one hundred "community-driven" master plans for Area C have been developed since 2011. The Quartet also announces that one hundred master plans for communities across Area C have been submitted to the Israeli authorities, but does not specify either time-frames for approval or other crucial details.

This paucity of information begs questions about how master plans are designed, by whom and for whom, and to what level "participation-planning" can help shape a grassroots, bottom-up plan to represent actual community needs. Participation-planning implies the active, free, and engaged participation of community members–minorities, women, elders, youth–in making

Israeli military and Border Police demolish houses in Area C. Image by 'Atef Abu a-Rub and Yusef Bani 'Odeh via B'Tselem/Wikimedia Commons.

critical decisions with respect to the shaping of local spaces and use of local resources. The implication that participation-planning is enforced within broader master-planning activities raises serious concerns about popular consent. A key issue with participation-planning processes in the occupied territories is that planners are working with an occupied population directly, and often at the level of individual and isolated communities. As a result, the community is often in a vulnerable position as it participates in critical decision-making processes. That participation can take place without full knowledge of potential risks towards the community, neighboring village or town, or the overall Palestinian territories in the long-term. Furthermore, by working at the community level to produce and re-produce elastic borders and territorial alignments, the system directly or indirectly aids in fragmenting Palestine. This process divests from any national aspiration to de-colonize historic Palestine. Instead, it engages in activities that produce smaller and more disconnected Palestinian communities.

One way to look at the entire occupation is to include the various aspects of how Israel exercises control over land and bodies. Area C, in particular, highlights the occupation's character, which seeks to consistently de-develop and displace Palestinian communities.

More seriously, as donors and other agents are aware, any master plan approved by the ICA will seriously disadvantage Palestinians at every level. The final plan frequently fails to include several sustainable features, including water networks, access to arable/agricultural lands, human and infrastructural development, or networks that connect one Palestinian community to another. Planning through the ICA process ends up shaping isolated, smaller, and disjointed communities surrounded by structures of the occupation, including check-points, settlements, the wall, and military zones or areas.

The PA maintains a passive-aggressive approach towards master-planning. It participates in the facilitation process of planning and design across Area C, while simultaneously stressing the importance of regaining control of the territory. To this end, both the PA and other international agents must consider the serious implications of master-planning. *First*, international humanitarian law is clear with respect to the 1967 border, and therefore both the occupation and its structures are deemed illegal and unlawful. *Second*, as the ICA is undoubtedly an extension of the occupation, its policies and practices are both unlawful and discriminatory towards Palestinians. Therefore there are critical risks in negotiating or fine-tuning ICA policies with respect to planning in the interest of Palestinians in Area C.

There are also serious short-term and long-term consequences of enforcing or participating in ICA-enforced planning regulations for Palestinian communities. A key threat includes making permanent illegal settlements inside the 1967 borders, and the displacement of communities from Area C to other parts of the occupied territories. A critical report produced by Diakonia lays out a comprehensive legal analysis, which identifies the Israeli planning regime as "inherently unlawful," discriminatory, and one that fails to respect and protect Palestinians and their properties as international law stipulates. The report states:

> It is worth reiterating that parties to the conflict must bear in mind at all times the inviolability of the rights of the protected Palestinian population, as stipulated by Article 47 of the Fourth Geneva Convention. The protection afforded to the Palestinian population cannot be undermined by any changes to the institutions or governments of the oPt, nor by any agreement between the authorities of the occupied territory and the occupying power. It should be noted in this regard, that the Interim Agreement on the West Bank and the Gaza Strip (including Annex III, Article 27: Planning and Zoning) cannot derogate from the fundamental protections granted to the protected population under the

law of occupation, and cannot serve to codify or justify an unlawful planning regime put in place by Israel; or explain the detrimental impediment on Palestinians in initiating, preparing, amending, and abrogating planning schemes, issuing building permits, and supervising and monitoring building activities.

International humanitarian law with respect to territorial changes clearly highlights that any changes made on the ground, policy, or local military law and practice cannot annul the protections safeguarded for Palestinians living under occupation. Thus, there is clear protocol for donors–PA and other civil society agents–to place pressure on Israel as the occupying power to enforce and implement the rights and responsibilities of an occupying power. As is made clear in international humanitarian law, Israel is obliged to administer the occupied territories, protect the local population, maintain law and order, and ensure that the rights and needs of the Palestinians under occupation are respected. Furthermore, in the context of prolonged occupation, the status of Palestinians as "protected persons" is far more serious. Both the occupation and the linked planning regime have continuously undermined that status.

One way to look at the entire occupation is to include the various aspects of how Israel exercises control over land and bodies. Area C, in particular, highlights the occupation's character, which seeks to consistently de-develop and displace Palestinian communities. Therefore, interventions which donors propose must be critical, direct, and clear in targeting the occupation's symptoms while constantly challenging it at its core
.

Recommendations and Proposed Approaches to Planning

In light of the violations which international law clearly identifies, donors funding planning initiatives and their implementing partners, including UN agencies, must immediately halt all such practices and recognize that any coordination around planning and zoning legitimizes the illegal Israeli occupation and its practices across the Palestinian territories. Serious efforts must be made toward challenging the Israeli occupation of the Palestinian territories by holding Israel accountable to its obligations as an occupying power as stipulated under international law. Moreover, the PA must ensure that any bilateral agreements with Israel do not concede the rights of Palestinians, including their right to sovereignty over natural resources.

With respect to the international assistance program operating in the Palestinian territories, both humanitarian and development organizations must revise their interventions and reflect whether their presence furthers or distracts from the national liberation project for historic Palestine. Often, this may mean making difficult decisions to neither negotiate nor coordinate with the occupation, and to put Palestinian needs and rights above all operational protocols. In Area C the situation is exceptionally dire, which is a clear indicator that the assistance program falls short of the needs of the local communities. Moreover, it is critical to hold Israel responsible for its duties as an occupying power. Currently, several curative and traditional models are being implemented across the Palestinian territories. With respect to Area C, donor and international engagement is limited and has

yet to deeply consider alternatives to drastically improve the living conditions of the local population.

Some questions that both planners and practitioners must reflecton include: how to critically respond and challenge the ICA planning regime, and how can interventions reverse and improve the livelihoods and development of Area C. Some interventions could respond to the conditions heightened military occupation in Area C creates. Some concrete tasks include filling the gaps for rural communities by providing access to subsidized or sustainable water networks, animal fodder, agricultural inputs, and other infrastructural necessities for people and livestock. Another possible measure is preparing for post-demolition relief, in order to respond immediately to protect Palestinians against displacement.

> *Serious efforts must be made toward challenging the Israeli occupation of the Palestinian territories by holding Israel accountable to its obligations as an occupying power as stipulated under international law.*

For example, recently, the Red Cross reportedly altered its post-demolition intervention under Israeli pressure. Ran Goldstein from the Red Cross confirmed that tents would no longer be provided to Jordan Valley residents in cases of post-demolition. Such decisions are detrimental to the cause and struggle of Palestinian communities facing displacement and other occupation-related risks. Moreover, the failure of humanitarian organizations to protect vulnerable communities calls into question their legitimacy and accountability to humanitarian law, commitment to universally accepted principles, and human rights. In order to reverse the current status of Palestinians in Area C, donors and other stakeholders must launch an active campaign to build the resilience of communities, instead of taking reactionary or submissive approaches that continue to perpetuate the occupation.

Finally, any donor-led master planning initiative that works under the framework of the ICA will continue to be misplaced in its attempt to build sustainable and viable communities. Therefore, donors and their partners must adopt a different approach: one that seeks to lobby against ICA control of planning across Area C, and restore authority to the Palestinians.

Endnotes:
1. Meron Benvenisti, *Judea and Samaria Lexicon* (Hebrew) (Jerusalem, 1987), 67-69.
2. Palestinian Central Bureau of Statistics (PCBS), *Labor Force Survey: Annual Report 2000, 2011* (Ramallah, Palestine).
3. Policy Briefing: "Area C: More than 60% of the occupied West Bank threatened by Israeli annexation," European Parliament Directorate- General for External Policies (April, 2013).
4. OCHA, *Al-Hadidiya Fact Sheet* (July, 2009).

Sexual Violence, Women's Bodies, and Israeli Settler Colonialism

JADMAG PEDAGOGY PUBLICATIONS ISSUE 4.1

Nadera Shalhoub-Kevorkian, Sarah Ihmoud and Suhad Dahir-Nashif

They not only invaded our home, took over our space, and evicted us—they even arrested me and took me to the Maskubya—the police station. I was put in room number four, alone, for a long time. Then, a big and tall man, a police officer, entered the interrogation room. I was alone, and started shivering from fear as he closed the door, started moving things around in the room and examining me from head to toe. I was terrorized, and my heart was beating so fast. His eyes penetrated my body, as he was opening the drawers looking for something. Then, he left the room and came back five minutes later holding a box. He pulled out a pair of blue plastic gloves, and put one on each of his hands, while looking at me and saying "Come here…" I must tell you that I was terrorized when they invaded the house and evicted us. I was extremely anxious when they arrested my son. However my fears of "you know what"…you know…being abused…being raped by his blue big hands and more…were the most terrifying moments of my life.[1]

These were the words of Sama, a thirty-six-year-old Palestinian woman who lost the intimate familial and physical space of her home, only to experience further terror with the threat of sexual abuse. Sama's narrative is not uncommon, as colonized women living under severe deprivation and dispossession are subject to daily attacks against their sexuality and bodily rights. Sexual violence is central to the larger structure of colonial power, its racialized machinery of domination, and its logic of elimination. This is readily apparent in the history of settler colonial contexts, where the machinery of violence explicitly targets native women's sexuality and bodily safety as biologized "internal enemies" since they are the producers of the next generation.

Settler colonialism as a "structure, not an event" operates through a "logic of elimination" that seeks to erase indigenous presence on a specific territory (settler colonialism's "irreducible element"). Settler colonialism "destroys in order to replace." The invasion of indigenous land seeks to permanently erase the indigenous presence on the land, in order to replace it with the new settler society and polity. Scholars have argued that settler colonialism's logic of elimination may culminate in indigenous genocide. In its European formations, both settler colonialism and genocide have "employed the organizing grammar of race." Since its inception, the Jewish state has been embedded in a racialized colonial logic. This logic constructs the Palestinian as a dangerous other in opposition to the white/Jewish subject and polis. As numerous authors have noted, this racial configuration

is articulated through early Zionist thinkers' orientalist ideology that framed the Jewish people as bearers of European civilization in the face of a culturally backward region and people. Such a "modernizing" project or "civilizing" mission relied on a Zionist imaginary of exclusively Jewish labor cultivating an empty, uncultivated land, and "making the desert bloom." Early Zionist leadership attempted to actualize the foundational Zionist myth of a "land without people for a people without land" through systematic ethnic cleansing of indigenous Palestinians in 1948. The Zionist entity continues to evict native Palestinians today. The massacres in Gaza of July-August 2014, and the repressive "iron fist" policies targeting Palestinian Jerusalemites at the time we write this article, are contemporary modes of settler colonial eviction of the Palestinian native.

Sexual violence is central to the larger structure of colonial power, its racialized machinery of domination, and its logic of elimination.

The targeting of Palestinian women's bodies and sexuality, we contend, is structural to the Israeli settler colonial project's racialized logic of elimination. Rape and other forms of sexual violence against Palestinian women have always been an element of the settler colonial state's attempts to destroy and eliminate indigenous Palestinians from their land. In addition to rape and other forms of sexual violence, the racialized logic of sexual violence energizes the very imaginary and project of conquering and cultivating Palestinian land, in transforming it into the Jewish polis. Hence, our discussion of sexual violence is embedded not only in the sexualized practices and politics of the Zionist state, but also in the nature of Israeli settler colonial violence itself.

As Palestinian feminists, we assert that the Zionist movement's imaginary of conquering and settling the Palestinian body is inseparable from the project of conquering and settling Palestinian land, and erasing indigenous presence. Here, we build on native scholar Andrea Smith's assertion that the logic of colonial sexual violence "establishes the ideology that Native bodies are inherently violable—and by extension, that Native lands are also inherently violable." It is the logic of settler colonial sexual violence that we center in our analysis of the continuous Nakba that targets our people. We trace the logic of sexual violence, in its historical and present context, as machinery, hidden and apparent, of colonial patriarchy against indigenous communities in Palestine. The logic of sexual violence attempts to fragment Palestinian family and communal life, as it severs the connection to the Palestinian homeland. The Zionist project is inherently based on the destruction of Palestinian native bodies and land, which cannot be separated from the colonial logic of elimination. Sexual violence is not simply a byproduct of colonialism, rather "colonialism is itself structured by the logic of sexual violence."

They not only invaded our home, took over our space, and evicted us—they even arrested me and took me to the Maskubya—the police station. I was put in room number four, alone, for a long time. Then, a big and tall man, a police officer, entered the interrogation room. I was alone, and started shivering from fear as he closed the door, started moving things around in the room and examining me from head to toe. I was terrorized, and my heart was beating so fast. His eyes penetrated my body, as he was opening the drawers looking for something. Then, he left the room and came back five minutes later holding a box. He pulled out a pair of blue plastic gloves, and put one on each of his hands, while looking at me and saying "Come here..." I must tell you that I was terrorized when they invaded the house and evicted us. I was extremely anxious when they arrested my son. However my fears of "you know what"...you know...being abused...being raped by his blue big hands and more...were the most terrifying moments of my life.[1]

These were the words of Sama, a thirty-six-year-old Palestinian woman who lost the intimate familial and physical space of her home, only to experience further terror with the threat of sexual abuse. Sama's narrative is not uncommon, as colonized women living under severe deprivation and dispossession are subject to daily attacks against their sexuality and bodily rights. Sexual violence is central to the larger structure of colonial power, its racialized machinery of domination, and its logic of elimination. This is readily apparent in the history of settler colonial contexts, where the machinery of violence explicitly targets native women's sexuality and bodily safety as biologized "internal enemies" since they are the producers of the next generation.

Settler colonialism as a "structure, not an event" operates through a "logic of elimination" that seeks to erase indigenous presence on a specific territory (settler colonialism's "irreducible element"). Settler colonialism "destroys in order to replace." The invasion of indigenous land seeks to permanently erase the indigenous presence on the land, in order to replace it with the new settler society and polity. Scholars have argued that settler colonialism's logic of elimination may culminate in indigenous genocide. In its European formations, both settler colonialism and genocide have "employed the organizing grammar of race." Since its inception, the Jewish state has been embedded in a racialized colonial logic. This logic constructs the Palestinian as a dangerous other in opposition to the white/Jewish subject and polis. As numerous authors have noted, this racial configuration is articulated through early Zionist thinkers' orientalist ideology that framed the Jewish people as bearers of European civilization in the face of a culturally backward region and people. Such a "modernizing" project or "civilizing" mission relied on a Zionist imaginary of exclusively Jewish labor cultivating an empty, uncultivated land, and "making the desert bloom." Early Zionist leadership attempted to actualize the foundational Zionist myth of a "land without people for a people without land" through systematic ethnic cleansing of indigenous Palestinians in 1948. The Zionist entity continues to evict native Palestinians today. The massacres in Gaza of July-August 2014, and the repressive "iron fist" policies targeting Palestinian Jerusalemites

at the time we write this article, are contemporary modes of settler colonial eviction of the Palestinian native.

The targeting of Palestinian women's bodies and sexuality, we contend, is structural to the Israeli settler colonial project's racialized logic of elimination. Rape and other forms of sexual violence against Palestinian women have always been an element of the settler colonial state's attempts to destroy and eliminate indigenous Palestinians from their land. In addition to rape and other forms of sexual violence, the racialized logic of sexual violence energizes the very imaginary and project of conquering and cultivating Palestinian land, in transforming it into the Jewish polis. Hence, our discussion of sexual violence is embedded not only in the sexualized practices and politics of the Zionist state, but also in the nature of Israeli settler colonial violence itself.

> *In addition to rape and other forms of sexual violence, the racialized logic of sexual violence energizes the very imaginary and project of conquering and cultivating Palestinian land, in transforming it into the Jewish polis.*

As Palestinian feminists, we assert that the Zionist movement's imaginary of conquering and settling the Palestinian body is inseparable from the project of conquering and settling Palestinian land, and erasing indigenous presence. Here, we build on native scholar Andrea Smith's assertion that the logic of colonial sexual violence "establishes the ideology that Native bodies are inherently violable—and by extension, that Native lands are also inherently violable." It is the logic of settler colonial sexual violence that we center in our analysis of the continuous Nakba that targets our people. We trace the logic of sexual violence, in its historical and present context, as machinery, hidden and apparent, of colonial patriarchy against indigenous communities in Palestine. The logic of sexual violence attempts to fragment Palestinian family and communal life, as it severs the connection to the Palestinian homeland. The Zionist project is inherently based on the destruction of Palestinian native bodies and land, which cannot be separated from the colonial logic of elimination. Sexual violence is not simply a byproduct of colonialism, rather "colonialism is itself structured by the logic of sexual violence."

Sexual Violence and Palestinian Genocide Since the Nakba

Understanding the intensified attacks on Palestinian women's bodies in times of heightened attacks by the settler colonial regime requires a feminist analysis. Such an analysis takes the Nakba as its analytical point of departure. Israel was built on the ruins of the Palestinian homeland, on its land, pain, and displacement. It was built on the destruction of our communal social ties, the violation and invasion of our homes and bodies.

Rape and killing of Palestinian women was a central aspect of Israeli troops' systematic massacres and evictions during the destruction of Palestinian villages in 1948. During the Deir Yassin massacre, for instance:

Deaths. Drawing by Suhad Daher-Nashif.

All the inhabitants were ordered into the village square. Here, they were lined up against a wall and shot. One eye-witness said her sister, who was nine months pregnant, was shot in the back of the neck. Her assailants then cut open her stomach with a butcher's knife and extracted the unborn baby. When an Arab woman tried to take the baby, she was shot…Women were raped before the eyes of their children before being murdered and dumped down the well.

David Ben Gurion, like other Zionist leaders, openly discussed the rape and sexual torture of Palestinian women in his diary entries during 1948. At the same time that he advocated the killing of Palestinian women and children, constructing them as a threat to the Jewish settler polity, he awarded a prize to every Jewish mother on her tenth child. Ben Gurion ensured that the Jewish Agency, not the state, administered such pronatal incentives in order to guarantee the exclusion of Arabs.[2] The fetishization of fertility has made Palestinians, especially women, targets of nationalist rhetoric that deeply politicizes their reproduction. For Zionists, Palestinian women have always been, and continue to be, as we have seen in the latest attacks on Gaza, targets of the Zionist killing machine.

Feminist scholars have also suggested that the Zionist state mobilizes violence against Palestinian women's bodies and sexuality to strengthen indigenous patriarchal structures and aid in the eviction of Palestinians from their land. Militarized sexual abuse has been rampant under Israeli occupation. The Israeli state and military forces have exploited the threat of sexual violence against Palestinian women, and patriarchal perceptions of sexuality and "honor" to "recruit Palestinians as collaborators" during periods of uprisings and deter attempts at organized resistance. This practice has been so historically prevalent that it gained its own term in the Arabic language as *isqat siyassy*, meaning the sexual abuse of Palestinians for political reasons. The state's security apparatus continues to use Palestinians' sexual identities and orientalist conceptions of "Arab culture" to recruit collaborators and fragment Palestinian society. Recent revelations by Israel's secret

military intelligence Unit 8200 have revisited this fact. The literal and figurative "rape" of Palestinian women's bodies, framed as inherently violable by the Zionist entity, is inherently structured by the same logic of sexual violence that energizes the settler colonial project's violation and continued confiscation of Palestinian natives' land.

Unmasking the Logic of Sexual Violence

The silence on the Zionist machinery's use of sexual violence against Palestinian women[3] and their communities has been further revealed since the inception of the state's most recent military operations. The logic of sexualized violence that structures the Israeli settler colonial project has become more visible during the last period of military invasion. Slogans such as "Death to Arabs" and "Arabs out" have become more usable and tolerable in the Israeli public sphere, exposing the necropolitical drive against Palestinian natives at the core of the so-called Jewish democracy.

On 1 July, just after discovery of the bodies of three Jewish settler youth who had gone missing in the occupied West Bank, Israeli professor Mordechai Kedar of the Begin-Sadat Center for Strategic Studies remarked on public radio: "the only deterrent for … those who kidnapped the [Israeli] children and killed them, the only way to deter them is their knowledge that either their sister or their mother will be raped if they are caught … this is the culture of the Middle East." His comments suggested that raping Palestinian women was the only deterrent to Palestinian resistance and "terrorism."

We as Palestinian feminists were not surprised to hear Kedar advocating rape as an antidote to anti-colonial resistance. Making such comments on public radio, in the open, where it would be heard by a wide Israeli Jewish public, women as well as men, including Israeli Jewish feminists, reflects the settler's mentality and socialization towards Palestinians. Discussing the rape of Palestinian women as a military strategy by a so-called scholar from one of the prominent universities in Israel reveals the mode in which colonizers portray colonized women. The presentation of a sexualized orientalist discourse positions Palestinians as culturally "backward," non-human others.

Lest the sexualized discourses Kedar mobilized appear an aberration, it is important to note that he was not the only performer in this latest theater of sexualized violence. Israeli soldiers on their way to killing Palestinians in Gaza read slogans of support prepared by their fellow Jewish-Israeli civilians stating: "Go pound their mothers, and come back to your mother." Israeli Jews gathered on hillsides to watch and cheer as the military dropped bombs on Gaza. One young Jewish woman's Facebook post summed up the sexualized pleasure they received in spectatorship of our collective lynching: "What an orgasm to see the Israeli Defense Forces bomb buildings in Gaza with children and families at the same time. Boom boom." Even their Prime Minister Netanyahu received a post, which circulated widely among the Israeli public via social media, showing a veiled woman labeled "Gaza," naked from the waist down, holding a message: "Bibi, finish inside this time! Signed, citizens in favor of a ground assault." This is in addition to Knesset member Ayelet Shaked's public declaration that Palestinian mothers should be killed.

The rape of the land as the rape of women's bodies has thus come to the fore in Israel's most recent eliminatory attacks against the Palestinian people. As the massacres of the Palestinian people in Gaza continued, the sexualized nature of the Israeli invasion and racial terror against Palestinian natives came to the forefront of nationalist politics and discussion among the public sphere within 1948 Palestine as well. Palestinian women took to the streets with their communities throughout historic Palestine to demonstrate against the continuous massacres in Gaza. Public demonstrations took a sexualized turn, as crowds' calls for "death to Arabs" quickly turned to chanting "Haneen Zoabi is a whore!" naming a female Palestinian member of the Israeli parliament who stood up for her people's right to life. Israeli police attacked Palestinian women's bodies, along with their male counterparts, and dragged them out of protests in Haifa and Nazareth, where they were arrested or beaten by racist crowds. Leading religious and military figures on the state's payroll issued religious edicts which stated that during times of war it is permissible to bomb Palestinian civilians in order to "exterminate the enemy." The city council of Or Yehuda, a settlement in Israel's coastal region, hung a banner supporting Israeli soldiers that suggested the rape of Palestinian women: "Israeli soldiers, the residents of Or Yehuda are with you! Pound their mother and come back home safely to your mother."[4]

Discussing the rape of Palestinian women as a military strategy by a so-called scholar from one of the prominent universities in Israel reveals the mode in which colonizers portray colonized women.

We argue that the logic of sexual violence exhibited during attacks on indigenous Palestinians throughout historic Palestine, both historically and during the Israeli state's most recent attacks, pervades both the Israeli settler state and settler society. Indeed, the state and settler society are inseparable entities, connected through a visceral psychological and political imaginary that exceeds the commonly framed state/civil society divide. As Lorenzo Veracini notes, settlers "carry their sovereignty with them." Both the state apparatuses (including public elected officials, academic and military institutions) and settler society (including Israeli publics—situated along the continuum of Zionist ideology) embody the machinery of settler colonial violence. It is no surprise then, that both the official state apparatuses and unofficial settler spheres have exhibited grave attacks on Palestinian women's sexuality, bodies, and lives in the context of the latest invasions of our people in Gaza, in the daily attacks today in Jerusalem, and throughout historic Palestine.

Israeli officials' repressive policies and incitement against the Palestinian people work to empower and embolden Israeli settler society to embody the power of the state and viciously attack Palestinians. This is clearly exhibited in the attacks on Palestin-

ian women's bodies inside al-Aqsa mosque these last weeks in Jerusalem, by both settler publics empowered by the state's military protection, and members of the state security forces. A recent example of the daily scene of sexual violence is Israeli border police's violent beating and arrest of Aida, a Palestinian woman from the old city of Jerusalem. When she tried to enter al-Aqsa mosque, border police attacked and brutally beat Aida. They tore off her hijab and pulled her by her hair, as they continued to beat her through the streets of the old city, and dragged her into the police car. She was then taken to the police station, where she was violently interrogated, further beaten and accused of attacking a police officer. Security forces' brutalization and violation of Aida's body, and attempts to mark her as an inherently criminal other, are a form of gendered and sexual violence. The legalization of such forms of violence marks the Israeli legal system itself as deeply embedded in the settler colonial project's machinery of elimination.

Palestinian women's brutalization and violation by the settler colonial state also takes on more mundane forms. When Samera was arrested for participating in a demonstration in occupied East Jerusalem, her release by authorities was conditional upon her completing what they termed "community service." Samera's "community service" required her to scrub the bathrooms of a facility for Israeli border police and soldiers. As she explained to us:

> I could not afford to pay the huge fine, and needed to be released [from prison] to go back to my kids. I had no other choice but to scrub their bathrooms....Just by being there, in men's bathrooms, in the Israeli men's toilets felt like rape. I did it to avoid payment, but I cannot avoid feeling that I allowed them to keep me there, in their bathrooms, in a constant state of terror, fearing being sexually abused, then trashed like we trash toilet paper in toilets.

Samera's words and analysis further illustrate the gendered and sexualized aspects of the complex machinery of settler colonial violence. Yet as Samera concluded: "Sometimes I feel I was their slave, but some other times I tell myself no, this is resistance, this is *sumud*, this is power...I did what was needed to come back to my children, without being touched or violated sexually....yes hard, complex...our situation is complex." Even in the face of such violent inscription of settler colonial violence, Palestinian women's daily acts of resistance and survival demonstrate their power and *sumud*, or steadfastness.

In sum, sexual and gender violence are not merely a tool of patriarchal control, the byproduct of war or intensified conflict. Colonial relationships are themselves gendered and sexualized. We contend that sexual violence, a logic embedded in the Israeli settler colonial project, follows two contradictory principles that operate simultaneously: invasion/violation/occupation and supremacy/purification/demarcation. That is, the Zionist settler colonial project's invasion, violation, and occupation of indigenous Palestinians' bodies, lives, and land is intimately intertwined with its demarcation of racialized geographical and physical boundaries between Jewish citizenry and Palestinian natives as well as attempts to "purify" the Jewish national body of the Palestinian body, which is framed as a biopolitical contaminant. It is thus that the logic of sexual violence, embedded in the Zionist regime, energizes historical and continuous attacks on Palestinian bodies and lives.

Thus our struggle for indigenous sovereignty within anti-colonial activism as feminists is necessarily situated in the protection of Palestinian women's bodily safety and sexuality, family, and communal right to life. It is a struggle against the hypermasculine Zionist military and settler apparatuses that frame Palestinian women as inherently threatening racialized others whose bodies must be violated and destroyed as the internal enemy and "reproducers of Palestinians." This logic is inseparable from the settler colonial logic of elimination.

As Palestinian feminists concerned about the safety of women's bodies and lives, the continuity of our people and our future generations, we call on local and international feminists to join our struggle, challenge the settler colonial culture of impunity, and raise their voices against the ongoing Israeli state crimes.

Endnotes:
1. This quote was taken from a group discussion with Palestinian women in Jerusalem, 2014.
2. In the 1950s Ben Gurion, as the first prime minister of Israel, turned the issue of women's fertility into national priority, arguing that "increasing the Jewish birthrate is a vital need for the existence of Israel" and that "a Jewish woman who does not bring at least four children into the world is defrauding the Jewish mission." See S. Sharoni (1995). *Gender and the Israeli-Palestinian Conflict: the Politics of Women's Resistance*. Syracuse University Press. Also see U. Davis & W. Lehn (1983). "And the Fund Still Lives: The Role of the Jewish International Fund in the Determination of Israel's Land Policies", *Journal of Palestine Studies*, Vol. 7 (4), p.3, at pp.4-6(1978).
3. While centering our analysis on Palestinian women, we also note the Zionist state's use of sexual violence as a tactic to curb the "demographic threat" over some Jewish women's bodies, including black women (from the Ethiopian community) and women from impoverished backgrounds. While attempting to curb the birth rates of black and/or poor Jewish women, a practice we analyze as connected to the racialized project of curbing Palestinian reproduction and life, Israel has simultaneously sought to increase European Jewish birth through modernized practices such as buying ovum for human reproductive cloning from poor, Eastern European women. Besides, the Israeli state suggested that the law for preventing human reproductive cloning (1999) had expired and many of Israel's physicians, politicians and social researchers are embracing this practice as yet another strategy for maintaining a Jewish demographic advantage on the land of Palestine.
4. In addition to the posts and declarations against Palestinian mothers, Jewish girls, and women encouraged men serving in the Israeli Occupation Forces by sending them semi-nude or pornographic pictures as an expression of love and support (see http://www.pitria.com/israeli-girls-support-zahal).

JADMAG PEDAGOGY PUBLICATIONS ISSUE 4.1

Can Palestinian Men be Victims? Gendering Israel's War on Gaza

Maya Mikdashi Every morning we wake up to an updated butcher's bill: one hundred, two hundred, four hundred, six hundred Palestinians killed by Israel's war apparatus as of this writing. These numbers gloss over many details: the majority of Gazans, one of the most populated and impoverished areas in the world, are refugees from other parts of historic Palestine. It is under a brutal siege, and there is nowhere to hide from Israel's onslaught. Before this "war," Gaza was a form of quarantine, a population held captive and colonized by Israel's ability to break international law with impunity. It is a population in a relationship of dependency—for food, for water, medicine, even for movement—with their colonizers. In the event of a ceasefire, Gaza will remain colonized, quarantined, and blockaded. It will remain an open-air prison, a mass refugee camp.

One detail about the dead, however, is repeated often in Western-based mass media: the vast majority of murdered Palestinians in Gaza are civilians—and sources say that a "disproportionate" number are women and children. The killing of women and children is horrific—but, in the reiteration of these disturbing facts, there is something missing: the public mourning of Palestinian men killed by Israel's war machine. In 1990, Cynthia Enloe[1] coined the term "womenandchildren" in order to think about the operationalization of gendered discourses to justify the first Gulf War. Today, we should be aware of how the trope of "womenandchildren" is circulating in relation to Gaza and to Palestine more broadly. This trope accomplishes many discursive feats, two of which are most prominent: the massifying of women and children into an undistinguishable group brought together by the "sameness" of gender and sex, and the reproduction of the male Palestinian body (and the male Arab body more generally) as always already dangerous. Thus, the status of male Palestinians (a designation that includes boys aged fifteen and up, and sometimes boys as young as thirteen) as "civilians" is always circumspect.

This gendering of Israel's war on Gaza is conversant with discourses of the War on Terror and, as Laleh Khalili has argued persuasively, counter-insurgency strategy and war-making more broadly. In this framework, the killing of women and girls and pre-teen and underage boys is to be marked, but boys and men are presumed guilty of what they *might* do if allowed to live their lives. Furthermore, these boys and men are potentially dangerous not only to the militaries that occupy them, but also to those womenandchildren who actually are civilians. The young boys, after all, may grow up to be violent extremists. Thus, kill the flesh—extinguish the potential.

Only within this logic can criticism of Israel's war on Gaza be answered, straight faced, with statements about the "fate" of women and homosexuals "under" Hamas. Recently, a spokesman for Israel answered Noura Erakat's condemnation of Israel's violation of international human rights by sharing this

gem of wisdom: "Hamas, they would not allow a young, liberal, secular woman to express her views like you do, ma'am. They would not allow my gay friends to express their sexuality freely." This statement aims to mobilize the gendered discourse of the War on Terror, a discourse that plays on the affective registers of US liberalism through a pandering to feminist and LGBTQ rights. This pandering allows Islamophobia and war to be manifested as a public and international good—after all, it is "we" who are defending the helpless from the ravages of Muslim and Arab men. Laleh Khalili has called this "the use of gendered 'telling' to distinguish those who are to be protected from those who are to be feared or destroyed." This discourse is so powerful that it does not need to rely on facts—it has in fact overridden and pre-determined them.

> *In Israel, men, settlers, and even soldiers are framed as victims of Palestinian terrorism and aggression. All are publicly mourned. In an almost direct reversal, Palestinian boys and men who have been the primary target of Israel, as evidenced by the population of political prisoners and targeted assassinations, are not seen by Western-based mainstream media as victims of Israeli terrorism and aggression.*

The Israeli war machine, much like the US war machine in Afghanistan or Iraq, does not protect Palestinian queers and women and children. It kills them, maims them, and dispossesses them alongside their loved ones—for the simple reason that they are Palestinian, and thus able to be killed with impunity while the world watches. Today, the difference between Palestinian womenandchildren and Palestinian men is not in the production of corpses, but rather in the circulation of those corpses within dominant and mainstream discursive frames that determine who can be publicly mourned as "victims" of Israel's war machine. Thus the sheer number of womenandchildren dead are enough to mobilize the US president and the United Nations to make statements "condemning" the violence—but the killing, imprisonment, and maiming of Palestinian men and boys in times of war and ceasefire goes uncited. In Israel, men, settlers, and even soldiers are framed as victims of Palestinian terrorism and aggression. All are publicly mourned. In an almost direct reversal, Palestinian boys and men who have been the primary target of Israel, as evidenced by the population of political prisoners and targeted assassinations, are *not* seen by Western-based mainstream media as victims of Israeli terrorism and aggression. Palestinians are put in the self-defeating position of having to fight to be recognized as human, to be recognized in death and in life as victims of Israeli policies and actions.

In Gaza There's a Boy. Artwork by Mazen Kerbaj.

For Israel, Palestinians serve as a reminder that there is an "other" there—an irritant, a stain, a conscious or subconscious understanding that one's ability to be a "Jewish nation-state" or "Jewish democracy" is inextricably tied to another's presence and/ or erasure.

As such, every Palestinian man, woman, and child is living within a discursive and material infrastructure that identifies and enumerates them, sequesters and quarantines them, occupies and divides them, disenfranchises and under-develops them, places them under siege and wages war on them with impunity. These practices of the everyday have ceased to shock us. Perhaps this is not surprising, given the erasure and normalcy of the slow death, genocide, structural violence, and dependency lived daily on Native American reservations or indigenous Australian territories. In fact, it is the normalization of Israeli settler colonialism that produces today's war on refugees living in an open-air prison in Gaza as a separate and condemnable "event." It is the success of settler colonialism that "Gaza" is spoken of as somehow apart and different than historic Palestine, that "the West Bank" and "Gaza" are two separate and seperatable entities, rather than one nation divided and exiled into separate territories by practices of colonialism. Today's war lies on a continuum with the everyday structural and informal violence faced by Palestinians living in Gaza, the West Bank, Jerusalem, or as Palestinian citizens of Israel: from resource monopolization and water shortages to home demolitions and checkpoints and settler-only roads and talks of population "transfer" to overflowing prisons and second class citizenship. Historic Palestine, from the river to the sea, is an Israeli settler colony at varying stages of success.

Palestinian men and women and children are one people—and they are a people living under siege and within settler colonial conditions. They should not be separated in death according to their genitalia, a separation that reproduces a hierarchy of victims and mournable deaths. Jewish Israelis (including soldiers and settlers) occupy the highest rungs of this macabre ladder, Palestinian men the lowest. This hierarchy is both racialized and gendered, a twinning that allows Palestinian womenandchildren to emerge and be publicly and internationally mourned only in spectacles of violence, or "war"—but never in the slow and muted deaths under settler colonial conditions—the temporality of the "ceasefire." To insist on publicly mourning all of the Palestinian dead, men and women and children—at moments of military invasion and during the everyday space of occupation and colonization— is to insist on their right to have been alive in the first place.

Sex is often thought of as an accident of birth: after all, we had no say in our development in utero. We did not get to offer an opinion when others decided that we had been born with a vagina (and were thus female) or born with a penis (and were thus male). Similarly, the original sin of over one million Gazans—the one that makes them available for killing, maiming, and homelessness from the air, ground, and sea—is having been born Palestinian. The word "Palestinian" produces them as a threat and as a target, while the words "man" and "woman" determines the way their death can circulate. Palestinians had no choice or say in being born Palestinian, under settler colonial conditions or in refugee camps scattered across nation state borders. They did not pick up and move to Gaza on their own volition. To paraphrase Malcolm X: They did not arrive or land in Israel. Israel arrived and landed on them.

The emphasis on the killing of womenandchildren, to the exclusion of Palestinian boys and men, further normalizes and erases the structures and successes of Israeli settler colonialism. "Civilians" and "non-combatants" are chosen. Men are always already suspicious, the possibility for violence encased in human flesh. The individual and personal extinguishing of female lives and the lives of children is massified and spoken of in statistics. Palestinians are framed as having the ability to choose whether they are a threat to Israel, and thus deserving of death, or not, and thus deserving of continued colonization clothed in the rubric of "ceasefire" or, even more elusively, "peace."

However, you do not have to pick up a gun in Palestine to be a revolutionary or an "enemy" of Israel. You do not have to protest or throw stones or fly flags to be dangerous. You do not have to rely on underground tunnels for food and cancer medication in order to be deemed part of the civilian infrastructure of terrorism. To be a threat to Israel is easy: You just have to be Palestinian.

Endnotes:

1. Enloe, Cynthia, "Womenandchildren: making feminist sense of the Persian Gulf Crisis," The Village Voice 25.9 (1990): 1990.

About The Authors

Mouin Rabbani is a contributing editor of the *Middle East Report* and has published and commented widely on Palestinian affairs and the Israeli-Palestinian conflict. He was a senior analyst of the Middle East with the International Crisis Group. Previously he worked as Palestine director of the Palestinian American Research Centre. He is co-editor of *Jadaliyya* ezine.

Joel Beinin is the Donald J. McLachlan professor of history and professor of Middle East history at Stanford University. His research and writing focus on modern and contemporary Egypt, Israel, Palestine, the Arab-Israeli conflict, political Islam, and US policy in the Middle East. Beinin has written or edited nine books, most recently *Social Movements, Mobilization, and Contestation in the Middle East and North Africa* (Stanford University Press, 2011), co-edited with Frédéric Vairel; *The Struggle for Worker Rights in Egypt* (Solidarity Center, 2010); and *Workers and Peasants in the Modern Middle East* (Cambridge University Press, 2001). His articles have been published in leading scholarly journals as well as *The Nation*, *Le Monde Diplomatique*, *Middle East Report*, *The Los Angeles Times*, *The San Francisco Chronicle*, *The San Jose Mercury News*, *The San Diego Union-Tribune*, *The Jordan Times*, *Asia Times*, and several blogs.

Nur Arafeh is the policy fellow of Al-Shabaka: The Palestinian Policy Network, and is a consultant at the Ibrahim Abu-Lughod Institute of International Studies at Birzeit University. She previously worked as an associate researcher at the Palestine Economic Policy Research Institute (MAS), and as a lecturer of economics at Al-Quds Bard Honors College, Al-Quds University. Nur has a dual BA degree in political science and economics from Sciences Po University (France) and Columbia University (United States), and holds an MPhil degree in Development Studies from the University of Cambridge (United Kingdom). Her main research interests include the political economy of development in the Middle East, sociology and politics of development, and economic forms of resistance.

Noura Erakat, a human rights attorney and writer, is an assistant professor at George Mason University and teaches international human rights law in the Middle East at Georgetown University. Prior to joining GMU's faculty, Noura was a Freedman teaching fellow at Temple University, Beasley School of Law and served as legal counsel for a congressional subcommittee in the House of Representatives, chaired by Congressman Dennis J. Kucinich. Noura helped organize several national formations including Arab Women Arising for Justice (AMWAJ) and the US Palestinian Community Network (USPCN). She is a board member of the Institute for Policy Studies, editorial committee member of the *Journal of Palestine Studies*, board member of the Arab Studies Institute, policy advisor of *Al-Shabaka*; founding member of the DC Palestinian Film and Arts Festival; and co-founding editor of *Jadaliyya*. Noura has appeared on programs with various networks, such as MSNBC, Fox News, Democracy Now!, BBC, NPR, and Al-Jazeera and published extensively in mainstream press media. Her scholarly publications include: "Overlapping Refugee Legal Regimes: Closing the Protection Gap During Secondary Forced Displacement," (*Oxford International Journal of Refugee Law*); "New Imminence in the Time of Obama: The Impact of Targeted Killing on the Law of Self-Defense," (*Arizona Law Review*); and "Whiteness as Property in Israel: Revival, Rehabilitation, and Removal," (*Harvard Journal of Ethnic and Racial Justice*, forthcoming). Follow her on Twitter: @4noura.

Tariq Dana is assistant professor of political science at Hebron University. He received his Ph.D. from the Scuola Superiore Sant'Anna, Italy, where his focus was on the transformation of Palestinian civil society from mass-based movements to neoliberal-oriented NGOs. During this period, he was PhD visiting fellow at School of Oriental and African Studies (SOAS). He has worked with many Palestinian and international NGOs and UN agencies in the occupied Palestinian territory, Africa, and Europe. His research interests include civil society, NGOs and social movements, neoliberalism, and globalization and state-building with a particular focus on Palestine.

Nuriya Oswald is the international advocacy officer at Al Mezan Center for Human Rights.

Max Ajl studies development sociology at Cornell University and has been published widely, including the *Middle East Report*, *Historical Materialism*, and *The Guardian*'s Comment is Free. He is a contributing editor at *Jacobin* and co-editor of *Jadaliyya*'s Palestine page. He is on Twitter as @maxajl.

Lamya Hussain is a PhD Candidate at SOAS with the Department of Development Studies. Her current research deals with the agriculture sector across "Area C" communities, to identify the shifts in production and resource allocation. Hussain is also the founder and board director of Refutrees, and editor with the *Journal of Internal Displacement* (JID), contributing towards both practical projects rooted in community-based initiatives and research.

Dr. Nadera Shalhoub-Kevorkian is a longtime anti-violence, native Palestinian feminist, activist, and scholar. She is the Lawrence D. Biele Chair in Law at the Faculty of Law-Institute of Criminology and the School of Social Work and Public Welfare at the Hebrew University of Jerusalem. Her research focuses on femicide and other forms of gendered violence, crimes of abuse of power in settler colonial contexts, surveillance, securitization and social control, and trauma and recovery in militarized and colonized zones. Dr. Shalhoub-Kevorkian's most recent book is titled *Militarization and Violence Against Women in Conflict Zones in the Middle East: The Palestinian Case Study* (Cambridge University Press, 2010). Her forthcoming book is titled *Security Theology, Surveillance and the Politics of Fear* (Cambridge University Press).

Sarah Ihmoud is a doctoral candidate in social/activist anthropology at the University of Texas at Austin. She is a Palestinian American Research Center fellow, a Wenner-Gren Foundation Fellow, and is currently conducting dissertation research on sexuality, intimacy, and settler colonialism in Palestine/Israel. Sarah previously researched indigenous women's organizing against feminicide and other forms of gender violence in post-war Guatemala.

Dr. Suhad Daher-Nashif is a lecturer and researcher at Al-Qasimi College for Education and Oranim College for Education. She holds a PhD in social-medical Anthropology from the Hebrew University of Jerusalem. Her current research focuses on practices of death within Palestinian society including femicide and suicide, and Palestinian women's experiences in Israel with higher education, civil service participation and access to justice. One of her most recent publications is "Femicide and Colonization: Between the Politics of Exclusion and the Culture of Control" (2013), published in *Violence Against Women* with Dr. Shalhoub-Kevorkian, and a co-authored report on Palestinian youth attitudes towards killing women, forthcoming in 2014 by Baladna youth organization and Kayan feminist organization.

Maya Mikdashi received her PhD from Columbia University's Department of Anthropology. She is co-director of the documentary film *About Baghdad*. Maya is currently a Mellon Postdoctural fellow at Rutgers University. She is co-founder/editor of *Jadaliyya* ezine.

Sara Roy is a senior research scholar at the Center for Middle Eastern Studies specializing in the Palestinian economy, Palestinian Islamism and the Israeli-Palestinian conflict. She is also co-chair of the Middle East Seminar, jointly sponsored by the Weatherhead Center for International Affairs and the Center for Middle Eastern Studies, and co-chair of the Middle East Forum at the Center for Middle Eastern Studies. Dr. Roy is the author of *The Gaza Strip: The Political Economy of De-development* (Institute for Palestine Studies, 1995, 2001, third edition forthcoming); *The Gaza Strip Survey* (The West Bank Data Base Project, 1986); *Failing Peace: Gaza and the Palestinian-Israeli Conflict* (Pluto Press, 2007); and editor of *The Economics of Middle East Peace: A Reassessment, Research in Middle East Economics, Volume 3* (Middle East Economic Association and JAI Press, 1999); and *Hamas and Civil Society in Gaza: Engaging the Islamist Social Sector* (Princeton University Press, 2011; 2014, with a new afterword). Additionally, she serves on the Advisory Council of American Near East Refugee Aid (ANERA), and has served as a consultant to international organizations, the US government, human rights organizations, private voluntary organizations, and private business groups working in the Middle East.

The **Editors**

Noura Erakat (biography above)

Tareq Radi is a graduate student in the Department of Development Studies at the School of Oriental and African Studies (SOAS). His research interests include political economy, class and state formation, and critical race theory. Tareq is a host for the audio journal Status, where he produces a regular segment entitled Reclaiming Academic Freedom. In addition to his academic pursuits, Tareq is a photographer and filmmaker. Prior to his studies at SOAS, he graduated with a B.S in Finance from George Mason University (GMU), where he was a founding member and chairman of GMU's Students Against Israeli Apartheid (SAIA).

JADMAG PEDAGOGY PUBLICATIONS ISSUE 4.1

Teacher's Guide

This pedagogical project aims to rehabilitate the question of Gaza within an Israeli settler-colonial framework. Israel first tried to occupy the Gaza Strip in 1956, but was forced to withdraw its forces in response to pressure from the Eisenhower administration after only four months. Later, when it occupied it in 1967, the Israeli Knesset endorsed the annexation of the Gaza Strip in a secret cabinet meeting shortly after the close of the 1967 War.

After repeated and failed attempts to pacify the native Palestinian population, Israel began to shift its policy towards the coastal enclave. Since 1991, it has isolated, de-developed, and contained the territory and its population. Israel intensified its policy during the Second Palestinian Uprising between 2000-2005, which culminated in unilateral withdrawal in 2005. While Israel has framed the withdrawal of its settler population and military installations as the termination of its occupation, it has maintained control of its air space, its seaports, its electro-magnetic sphere, and its population registry, as well as the entry and exit of all goods and people. Legal scholars as well as the International Criminal Court, in dicta, have argued that Israel's ongoing authority amounts to effective control and thus its ongoing role as an occupying power. In contrast, since 2005, Israel has treated the Gaza Strip as a sui generis entity: it is neither occupied territory nor is it an independent state, it is a "hostile entity" unlike anything else that exists. This framing has had manifold ramifications.

In practice, Israel has adopted intermittent counterinsurgency campaigns aimed at diminishing the capacity of the captive Palestinian population to militarily resist Israel's structural violence. Conceptually, it has set Gaza apart from the rest of the Palestinian-Israel conflict so that there is no continuity between Israel's wars waged upon it and its treatment of Palestinians throughout Israel as well as the West Bank, including East Jerusalem.

Together, the practice of systematic war and the framework of unique distinction have set the Gaza Strip apart from the question of Palestine and transformed it into a national security question. By emphasizing the role of Hamas and diminishing the question of Palestine, Israel has collapsed conditions in Gaza with asymmetric conflicts, or what has come to be known as the "global war on terror," thus eliding the consequential distinctions between Palestinians and other non-state actors. This pedagogical project is an attempt to re-frame the issue in order to place greater emphasis on the broader question of Palestine and to explain Israel's policy toward the Gaza Strip in that context.

The following Teaching Guide is comprised of four parts: 1) History of Israel-Palestine; 2) Settler Colonialism; 3) Situating Gaza; and 4) Structural Violence.

Each part can be taught separately along with one of the film's four parts. Alternatively, it can be taught as a single unit in the course of one class or workshop to understand the conflict with a particular emphasis on the Gaza Strip.

Due to the spectacle and horror of warfare, lay audiences may be more familiar with Israel's repeated military operations, making Gaza a gateway to understanding the broader Palestinian-Israeli conflict. The materials below can be used together and/or separately and can be supplemented using the Bibliography as well as the JadMag.

Part I: Settler Colonialism
[To be paired with Part 2 of film]

Lesson Objectives & Pedagogical Goals
- Define and understand settler-colonialism; distinguish it from colonialism.

- Understand how Israel and Palestinians is a case study of settler-colonialism by understanding Palestinian presence and claims for a nation-state as well as the rise of Zionism as a Jewish nationalist movement.

- Draw parallels between Israel's treatment of Palestinians across various jurisdictions i.e., civil, military occupation, counterinsurgency.

Suggested Reading List & Resources
- Adalah, the Legal Center for Arab Minority Rights in Israel, "Umm al Heiran Unrecognized Village v. Hiran Settlement," YouTube video, 4:43. Posted February 2013. https://www.youtube.com/watch?v=FlgU6oLswv0.

- Brenda Bhandar and Rafeef Ziadah, "Acts and Omissions: Framing Settler Colonialism in Palestine Studies," *Jadaliyya*, 14 January, 2016. http://www.jadaliyya.com/pages/index/23569/acts-and-omissions_framing-settlercolonialism-in-.

- Caroline Elkins and Susan Pederson, "Settler-Colonialism: A Concept and Its Uses," *Settler Colonialism in the Twentieth Century*, edited by Caroline Elkins and Susan Pederson, (New York: Routledge, 2005) 1-20.

- Omar Jabary Salamanca, Mezna Qato, Kareem Rabie, and Sobhi Samour. "Introduction, Past is Present: Settler Colonialism in Palestine." *Settler colonial studies*, 2, no. 1 (2012) 1-8. https://www.academia.edu/9101689/Past_is_Present_Settler_Colonialism_in_Palestine.

- Patrick Wolfe, "Settler Colonialism and the Elimination of the Native," *Journal of Genocide Research*, 8, no. 4 (2006): 387-409.

- Additional References:
  - Adalah, the Legal Center for Arab Minority Rights in Israel. "Discriminatory Laws Database." http://www.adalah.org/en/content/view/7771.

  - Ahmad Amara, "The Negev Land Question: Between Denial and Recognition," *Journal of Palestine Studies*, 42, no. 4 (2013) 27-47. http://www.palestinestudies.org/jps/fulltext/162935.

  - Office for the Coordination of Humanitarian Affairs (OCHA), occupied Palestinian territories (oPt). Humanitarian Atlas 2015. United Nations, 2015. https://www.ochaopt.org/documents/atlas_2015_web.pdf.

  - Visualizing Palestine (infographics on various Israeli jurisdictions and resource allocation)

Suggested Discussion Questions
- What is settler-colonialism? How is it different from colonialism?

- How do the tripartite elements of dispossession, removal, and containment facilitate settler-colonialism? How does Israel achieve these goals in each of its jurisdictions of control: within Israel? Within the West Bank? Within the Gaza Strip?

- What is the Prawer Plan? Where is it taking place? How is it similar and different from settlement expansion in the West Bank?

- What is Israel's "Palestine problem"? How is the Israeli government solving this "problem"?

Suggested Activities
- Break the class up into groups of two to three and assign the class a settler-colonial case study. Suggestions include: the United States, Australia, Canada, Algeria, and South Africa. Ask them to answer the following questions for their case studies before returning to the group to share their responses and de-brief their findings.

  - Who are the native people?

  - Who are the settlers and what are their claims to the land?

  - What happened to the native population and how?

  - What are the native people's outstanding claims?

- What happened to the settlers?

- What are the similarities and differences between your case study and that of Israel and the Palestinians?

Part II: History of Israel Palestine
[To be paired with Part 3 of film]

Lesson Objectives & Pedagogical Goals
- Understand Israel's methods of control of Palestinian population across its jurisdictional authority and what explains its pursuit of different policies.

- Trace and contextualize historical trajectory of events and isolation of Gaza and examine Israel's rhetorical use of self-defense as an argument in light of Hamas's establishment in 1988 and its use of force.

- Understand that the West Bank and the Gaza Strip are slated to be the Palestinian state under the Palestinian-Israeli Peace Process. Explore the inherent challenges to the establishment of such a sovereign state in light of their non-contiguous territorial character and Israel's policy goal of autonomy for Palestinians rather than self-determination and sovereignty.

Suggested Reading List & Resources
- Joel Beinin and Lisa Hajjar, "Palestine, Israel, and the Arab-Israeli Conflict: A Primer," Middle East Research & Information Project, February 2014. http://www.merip.org/sites/default/files/Primer_on_PalestineIsrael(MERIP_February2014)final.pdf.

- Tariq Dana, "The Palestinian Capitalists that Have Gone Too Far," Al-Shabaka, 14 January 2014. https://al-shabaka.org/briefs/palestinian-capitalists-have-gonetoo-far/.

- Jean-Pierre Filiu, "One Palestine against Another," in Gaza: A History, (New York: Oxford University Press, 2014) 279-310.

- James Gelvin, "Israel, the Arab States and the Palestinians," in *The Modern Middle East* (Third Edition), (New York: Oxford University Press, 2011) 283-293.

- Darryl Li, "A Separate Piece?: Gaza and the 'No-State Solution'," *Jadaliyya*, 4 December 2012. http://www.jadaliyya.com/pages/index/8762/aseparate-piece_gaza-and-the-%E2%80%9Cno-state-solution%E2%80%9D-.

- Ilan Pappe, "The Drive for An Exclusively Jewish State," in *The Ethnic Cleansing of Palestine*, (Oxford: Oneworld Publications, 2006) 10-28.

- Sara Roy, "De-Development Revisited: Palestinian Economy and Society since Oslo," *Journal of Palestine Studies*, 28, no. 3 (1999) 64-82. http://duncankennedy.net/documents/Is-Pal/Second-Syllabus/Sara_Roy_De-Development_Revisited.pdf.

- Alaa Tartir,, "The Evolution and Reform of Palestinian Security Forces 1993-2013," *Stability: International Journal of Security and Development*, 4, no. 1 (2015). Accessed 5 June 2016. http://www.stabilityjournal.org/articles/10.5334/sta.gi/.

• Timeline from Gaza in Context, http://gazaincontext.weebly.com/gicslides.html.

Suggested Discussion Questions

• Where is the West Bank and what is its relationship to the Gaza Strip? Why does Israel want the West Bank? Why does it no longer desire the Gaza Strip?

• What are the Dayton Security Forces in the West Bank? Who trains and funds them? Who are they expected to protect and why? Why are there no Dayton Forces in the Gaza Strip?

• How has Israel de-developed and isolated the Gaza Strip since 1993? Why is that year particularly significant?

• When did Hamas launch its first suicide attack? When did Hamas launch its first rocket into Israel? What does the chronology of these attacks tell us about Israel's claims for the use of force against Palestinians in the Gaza Strip and beyond?

Suggested Activities

• Break the class into two to three groups and ask them each to answer the following questions:

  • What happened in 2006 and 2007 between Fatah and Hamas?

  • How did this impact the conflict, specifically Palestinian claims for liberation and Israeli military action?

  • How did the Palestinian leadership's policies in the West Bank aim to fulfill Israel's demands? Were they successful in meeting those demands? Did their compliance lead to benefit for the Palestinians?

• Imagine you were born in Gaza in 1986 and you are now thirty years old. What are the pivotal events in your life as someone living in the Gaza Strip?

  • Point to specific years and explain what happened, with the impact this had on you and your family.

Part III: Situating Gaza

[To be paired with Part 1 of film]

Lesson Objectives & Pedagogical Goals

• Place Gaza both geographically and conceptually—understand where it is and start to identify what makes it both similar to the rest of Palestine and unique in its experience.

• Define asymmetry in warfare-understand how asymmetry applies to Israel and Palestinians.

• Question how media affects our understanding of power and conflict.

Suggested Reading List & Resources

• Jehad Abusalim, "From Fence to Fence: Retelling Gaza's Story," in *Gaza as Metaphor*, edited by Dina Matar and Helga Tawil-Souri, (London: Hurst Publishers, 2016) 83-93.

• Basil Baker, "Interview with Dr. Basil Baker: Quick Death under Siege," by Nehad Khader. *Journal of Palestine Studies*, 44, no. 1 (2014) 126-132.

• Ilana Feldman Feldman, "Government Practice and the Place of Gaza," in *Governing Gaza*, (Durham: Duke University Press, 2008) 1-30.

• Ayman Mohyeldin, "Mediating the Assault on Gaza," by Adel Iskandar, *Status*, 1, no. 1 (2014). http:// www.statushour.com/aymanmohyeldin.html.

• Sherene Seikaly, "Gaza as Archive," in *Gaza As Metaphor*, edited by Dina Matar and Helga Tawil-Souri, (London: Hurst Publishers, 2016) 225-231.

• Nathan Thrall, "Hamas's Chances," *London Review of Books*, 36, no. 16 (2014): 10-12. http://www.lrb.co.uk/v36/n16/ nathan-thrall/hamass-chances. http://www.lrb.co.uk/v36/n16/ nathan-thrall/hamass-chances.

• References:

  • Institute for Middle East Understanding, "50 Days of Death & Destruction: Israel's 'Operation Protective Edge.'" 10 September 2014.

  • Office for the Coordination of Humanitarian Affairs (OCHA), occupied Palestinian territories (oPt).Gaza situation maps. United Nations. https:// www.ochaopt.org/maps.

  • OCHA, oPt. Humanitarian Atlas 2015. United Nations, 2015. https://www.ochaopt.org/ documents/atlas_2015_web.pdf.

  • Visualizing Palestine. Gaza's Untold Story: From Displacement to Death. http:// visualizingpalestine.org/visuals/ gaza-refugee-deaths. (visual)

  • Visualizing Palestine. Israeli & Palestinian Ceasefire Violations. http://visualizingpalestine.org/ visuals/gaza-ceasefire-violations. (visual)

Suggested Discussion Questions

• Where is the Gaza Strip? What is it: a state? An occupied territory? Something in between?

• What is Hamas? When was it founded? How many members does it have? Who are the Palestinians in the Gaza Strip?

- How did Israel try to pacify the population of Gaza and fail?

- Who has the right to self-defense? People or states and what is the difference?

Suggested Activities

- Word association and discussion framing. Begin an open discussion with a word association exercise (you could do this before and/or after viewing the video as a class) by asking students to say the first word that comes to mind when they hear "Gaza" or "Palestinians"

  - This can be done popcorn-style with whoever wants to participate or round robin until everyone has gone and students are satisfied with the words that have been listed on the board. Leave this list of words up for the remainder of the class as you conduct other activities and discussion based on the video and readings (if you are doing this over more than one class, take a photo of the words from the first day).

  - Come back to these words at the end of your lesson(s) and have students reflect on why certain words are on the board. Are there words they would remove? Are there words they would add? Why?

- **Media Analysis**

  - In groups of two to three, students read silently and then discuss one of the *New York Times* articles suggested below. Each group can/should be given a different article to help enrich the report-back to the rest of the class. For some of these articles, it is more helpful to conduct an analysis of the content or text; whereas, for others, it will be an analysis of the headline and larger framing. The level of guidance to students can be left to the instructor's discretion and can be very structured or can be an approach that allows them to bring back and tie their own reflections based on earlier readings or class discussion.

  - For groups conducting a textual analysis, names of the parties (states, political parties, etc.) involved should be blacked out and students should characterize/ describe each party based on the information and adjectives given in the article. For groups focusing on headlines or larger framing, no details need to be marked out.

  - Students should reflect on the following in their group discussions:

    - How does the article define self-defense through its narrative? Are there problems with this definition? Why?

    - What words/terms are used to describe the event? Are these "neutral" words or do they some kind of bias?

    - What words/terms are missing?

- What weapons or threats are included? Who is being threatened?

1. "Boys Drawn to Gaza Beach, and Into Center of Mideast Strife" (Original title: "Gaza Strip Beach Explosion Kills Children") http:// www.nytimes.com/2014/07/17/ world/ middleeast/gaza-stripbeach-explosion-killschildren.html

2. "A Growing Arsenal of Homegrown Rockets Encounters Israel's Iron Dome" http:// www.nytimes.com/2014/07/10/ world/middleeast/israel-gazamissiles-iron-dome.html

3. "Israelis Watch Bombs Drop on Gaza from Front-Row Seats" http://www.nytimes.com/ 2014/07/15/world/middleeast/ israelis-watch-bombs-drop-ongaza-from-front-row-seats.html

4. Video: "Cutting the Grass" http://www.nytimes.com/ video/ world/middleeast/ 100000002989054/cutting-thegrass-of-hamass-militancy.html

5. "Air Sirens Puncture Life in Affluent Tel Aviv Suburbs" http://www.nytimes.com/ 2014/07/10/world/middleeast/ israel-gaza-hamas-tel-avivpalestinians-iron-domerockets.html

6. "In Rubble of Gaza Seaside Café, Hunt for Victims Who Had Come for Soccer" http://www.nytimes.com/2014/07/11/ world/middleeast/missile-atbeachside-gaza-cafe-findspatrons-poised-for-worldcup.html?partner=rss&emc=rss&smid=twnytimes (See also, the original headline: "Missile at Beachside Café Finds Patrons Poised for World Cup." https://twitter.com/ nytimes/status/ 487334827931471873)

Part IV: Structural Violence
[To be paired with Part 4 of film]

Lesson Objectives & Pedagogical Goals

- Understand the meaning of structural violence and how the status quo can be a violent experience for marginalized populations.

- Understand how the concept of structural violence applies to Palestinians.

- Critically examine the responsibility of individuals and states in cases of conflict.

Suggested Reading List & Resources

- Max Ajl, "The Limits of Humanitarianism," *Jadaliyya*, 7 July 2015 http://www.jadaliyya.com/pages/index/22091/ the-limits-ofhumanitarianism.

- Noura Erakat, Bianca Isais, and Salmah Rizvi. "Operation Protective Edge & Legal Remedies," International Affairs & the UN in the Arab World Program Working Paper Series #24 (October 2014). https://www.aub.edu.lb/ifi/publications/ Documents/working_papers/ 20141009_noura_erakat.pdf.

- Samera Esmeir, "Colonial Experiments in Gaza." *Jadaliyya*, 14 July 2014. http://www.jadaliyya.com/pages/index/8482/

colonial-experiments-in-gaza-.

- Paul Farmer, "On Suffering and Structural Violence: A View from Below," *Daedalus*, 125, no. 1 (1996) 261-83.

- Rashid Khalidi, "Collective Punishment in Gaza," *The New Yorker*, 29 July 2014. http://www.newyorker.com/news/ newsdesk/collective-punishment-gaza.

- Mark Landler, "Gaza War Strains Relations Between the U.S., Israel," *New York Times*, 4 August 2014. http://www. nytimes.com/2014/08/05/world/middleeast/gaza-is-strain- ing-us-ties-to-israel.html.

- Nuriya Oswald, "Gaza Reconstruction Mechanism: Profiting Israel, Entrenching the Blockade," *Jadaliyya*, 7 July 2015. http://www.jadaliyya.com/pages/index/22089/gaza-recon- structionmechanism_profiting-israel-ent.

- Nicolas Pelham, "The Role of the Tunnel Economy in Rede- veloping Gaza," in *Decolonizing Palestinian Political Econ- omy: De-development and Beyond*, edited by Mandy Turner and Omar Shweiki, (New York: Palgrave Macmillan, 2014) 200-219.

- Mouin Rabbani, "Why the Gaza Truce Failed," *Jadaliyya*, 24 August 2014. http://www.jadaliyya.com/pages/index/ 18976/why-the-gaza-truce-failed.

Suggested Discussion Questions

- If there are no more military confrontations between Israel and the Palestinians, particularly Hamas, how will this affect the Israeli economy? The Israeli military? How will the lives of the Palestinians in the Gaza Strip be changed? What will happen to Palestinians in the West Bank, including East Je- rusalem? What will happen to Palestinian citizens of Israel?

- How long has Israel's siege on the Gaza Strip been in place? What does Israel claim it is meant to do? What does it do in practice? What is the humanitarian function of the tunnels in this context?

- What choices do Palestinians in the Gaza Strip have? What choices do Israelis have?

- What is the responsibility of the United States in this conflict? What is the responsibility of individuals? Of other countries or international organizations, such as the United Nations?

Suggested Activities

- Break the class up into groups of two to three and ask them to do one of two activities:

    1. Look at the terms of the 2012 and 2014 Israel-Palestin- ian Ceasefire agreements (below) and answer:

    - How similar are they?

    - Do they address the root of the conflict? Why or why

not?

- Will they successfully prevent another military con- frontation between Hamas and Israel? (For 2012 terms, see: http://www.haaretz.com/israel-news/ text-cease-fire-agreementbetween-israel-andhamas. premium-1.479653; For 2014 terms, see: http://www. bbc.com/news/worldmiddle-east-28939350; See also Hamas' terms for a desired ten-year truce: http:// www.bbc.com/ news/world-middleeast-28939350)

2. Ask the students to examine the claims of the global movement for boycott, divestment, and sanctions and answer:

- What are the demands of the BDS movement?

- Do these demands address the root cause of conflict?

- If the BDS Movement's three demands are success- fully implemented, will that help prevent another mil- itary confrontation between Hamas and Israel? If not, what value does it have, if any? (For BDS demands, see: https:// bdsmovement.net/bdsintro)

Other Resources

Books

Refaat Alareer, *Gaza Writes Back: Short Stories from Young Writers in Gaza, Palestine* (Charlottesville: Just World Books, 2014).

Max Blumenthal, *Goliath: Life and Loathing in Greater Israel* (New York, NY: Nation Books, 2014).

David B. Brooks and Stephen C. Lonergan. *Watershed: the Role of Freshwater in the Israeli-Palestinian Conflict* (Ottawa: International Development Research Centre, 1995).

Laila El-Haddad, *Gaza Mom Abridged Edition* (Charlottesville: Just World Books, 2013).

Laila El-Haddad and Maggie Schmitt, *The Gaza Kitchen: A Palestinian Culinary Journey* (Charlottesville: Just World Books, 2013).

Caroline Elkins and Susan Pederson, *Settler Colonialism in the Twentieth Century* (New York: Routledge, 2005).

Leila Farsakh, *Palestinian Labour Migration to Israel: Labour, Land and Occupation* (Routledge Political Economy of the Middle East and North Africa) (New York: Routledge, 2005).

Ilana Feldman, *Governing Gaza* (Durham: Duke University Press, 2008).

Jean-Pierre Filiu, *Gaza: A History* (New York: Oxford University Press, 2014).

James Gelvin, *The Modern Middle East* (Third Edition) (New York: Oxford University Press, 2011).

Gershom Gorenberg, *The Accidental Empire: Israel and the Birth of the Settlements, 1967-1977* (New York: Times Books, 2006).

Lisa Hajjar, *Courting Conflict: The Israeli Military Court System in the West Bank and Gaza* (Oakland: University of California Press, 2005).

Rashid Khalidi, *The Iron Cage: The Story of the Palestinian Struggle for Statehood* (Boston: Beacon Press, 2006).

Alex Lubin, *Geographies of Liberation: The Making of an Afro-Arab Political Imaginary* (Chapel Hill: University of North Carolina Press, 2014).

Ilan Pappe, *The Ethnic Cleansing of Palestine* (Oxford: One-

world Publications, 2006).

Avi Raz, *The Bride and the Dowry: Israel, Jordan, and the Palestinians in the Aftermath of the June 1967 War* (New Haven: Yale University Press, 2012).

Shira Robinson, *Citizen Strangers: Palestinians and the Birth of Israel's Liberal Settler State* (Stanford: Stanford University Press, 2013).

Sara Roy, *Hamas and Civil Society in Gaza* (Princeton: Princeton University Press, 2013).

Edward Said, *Peace And Its Discontents: Essays on Palestine in the Middle East Peace Process* (New York, NY: Vintage, 1996).

Sherene Seikaly, *Men of Capital: Scarcity and Economy in Mandate Palestine* (Stanford: Stanford University Press, 2015).

Natalie Tabar and Grazia Careccia, *The Jerusalem Trap: The Looming Threat Posed by Israel's Annexationist Policies in Occupied East Jerusalem* (Ramallah: Al-Haq, 2010).

Chapters in Anthology

Jehad Abusalim, "From Fence to Fence: Retelling Gaza's Story," In *Gaza as Metaphor*, edited by Dina Matar and Helga Tawil-Souri (London: Hurst Publishers, 2016), 83-93.

Nicolas Pelham, "The Role of the Tunnel Economy in Redeveloping Gaza," in *Decolonizing Palestinian Political Economy: De-development and Beyond*, edited by Mandy Turner and Omar Shweiki (New York: Palgrave Macmillan, 2014), 200-219.

Sherene Seikaly, "Gaza as Archive," in *Gaza As Metaphor*, edited by Dina Matar and Helga Tawil-Souri (London:Hurst Publishers, 2016), 225-231.

Articles

News

Amnon Brazili, "For Peres — Yet Another Vision," In *Report on Israeli Settlement in the Occupied Territories* 5.1, listed as "How Peres Sees the Future," edited by Geoffrey Aronson, 2. Foundation for Middle East Peace: January 1995. http://fmep.org/wp/wp-content/uploads/1995/01/5.1.pdf.

Chris Hedges, "Arafat and Peres Confer on Accord," *New York Times*, 10 December 1993. http://www.nytimes.com/1993/12/10/world/arafat-and-peres-confer-on-accord.html.

Amanda Macias, Jeremy Bender, and Skye Gould. "The 35 Most Powerful Militaries in the World," *Business Insider*, 10 December 2014. http://www.businessinsider.com/the-worlds-most-powerful-militaries-2014-12.

Ari Shavit, "The Enemy Within," *Haaretz*, 29 August 2002. http://www.haaretz.com/the-enemy-within-1.35604.

Tracy Wilkinson, "Palestinians' New Weapon: Mortars; Israel Reports 56 Ariel Attacks in Recent Months The Small Canons Have a Range of 2 1/2 Miles," *Contra Costa Times* (California), 10 April 2001.

Essays

Ali Abunimah, ""Gaza Is a Graveyard," Sing Joyful Israeli Youths," *Electronic Intifada*, 28 July 2014. https://electronicintifada.net/blogs/ali-abunimah/gaza-graveyard-sing-joyful-israeli-youths.

Brenda Bhandar and Rafeef Ziadah, "Acts and Omissions: Framing Settler-Colonialism in Palestine Studies," *Jadaliyya*, 14 January 2016. http://www.jadaliyya.com/pages/index/23569/acts-and-omissions_framing-settler-colonialism-in-

Tariq Dana, "The Beginning of the End of Palestinian Security Coordination with Israel?" *Jadaliyya*, 4 July 2014. http://www.jadaliyya.com/pages/index/18379.

Tariq Dana, "The Palestinian Capitalists that Have Gone Too Far," *Al-Shabaka*, 14 January 2014. https://al-shabaka.org/briefs/palestinian-capitalists-have-gone-too-far/.

Noura Erakat, "Israel Will Invade Gaza Again—the Only Question Is How Soon," *The Nation*. 8 July 2015. http://www.thenation.com/article/israel-will-invade-gaza-again-the-only-question-is-how-soon.

Noura Erakat, "Permission to Kill in Gaza," *Jadaliyya*, 7 July 2015. http://www.jadaliyya.com/pages/index/22093/permission-to-kill-in-gaza.

Samera Esmeir, "Colonial Experiments in Gaza," *Jadaliyya*, 14 July 2014. http://www.jadaliyya.com/pages/index/8482/colonial-experiments-in-gaza-.

Human Rights Watch, "Israel: In-Depth Look at Gaza School Attacks," 11 September 2014. https://www.hrw.org/news/2014/09/11/israel-depth-look-gaza-school-attacks.

Lamya Hussain, "Planning under Occupation: Elastic Geographies and 'Area C,'" *Jadaliyya*, 16 July 2015. http://www.jadaliyya.com/pages/index/22193/planning-under-occupation_elastic-geographies-and-.

Rashid Khalidi, "Collective Punishment in Gaza," *The New Yorker*, 29 July 2014. http://www.newyorker.com/news/news-desk/collective-punishment-gaza.

Mark Landler, "Gaza War Strains Relations Between the U.S.,

Israel," *New York Times*, 4 August 2014. http://www.nytimes.com/2014/08/05/world/middleeast/gaza-is-straining-us-ties-to-israel.html?_r=0.

Darryl Li, "A Separate Piece?: Gaza and the "No-State Solution"," *Jadaliyya*, 4 December 2012. http://www.jadaliyya.com/pages/index/8762/a-separate-piece_gaza-and-the-%E2%80%9C-no-state-solution%E2%80%9D.

Maya Mikdashi, "Can Palestinian Men be Victims? Gendering Israel's War on Gaza," *Jadaliyya*, 23 July 2014. http://www.jadaliyya.com/pages/index/18644/can-palestinian-men-be-victims-gendering-israels-w.

Steve Niva, "Israel's 'Operation Mow the Lawn'," *Middle East Research and Information Project*, 7 December 2012. http://www.merip.org/israels-operation-mow-lawn.

Nuriya Oswald, "Gaza Reconstruction Mechanism: Profiting Israel, Entrenching the Blockade," *Jadaliyya*, 7 July 2015. http://www.jadaliyya.com/pages/index/22089/gaza-reconstruction-mechanism_profiting-israel-ent.

Mouin Rabbani, "Another Palestinian Uprising?" *Jadaliyya*, 7 August 2015. http://www.jadaliyya.com/pages/index/22365/another-palestinian-uprising.

Mouin Rabbani, "Why the Gaza Truce Failed," *Jadaliyya*, 24 August 2014. http://www.jadaliyya.com/pages/index/18976/why-the-gaza-truce-failed.

Scott Ratner, "There is no coexistence with cancer': Right-wing Israelis demand gov't give military 'free hand' to fight Palestinians," *Mondoweiss*, 9 October 2015. http://mondoweiss.net/2015/10/existence-military-palestinians/#sthash.ej3icDpd.dpuf.

Sara Roy, "Rebuilding Gaza Needs Freedom and Normality – Not Just Aid," *Jadaliyya*, 7 July 2015. http://www.jadaliyya.com/pages/index/22098/rebuilding-gaza-needs-freedom-and-normality_-not-j.

Nadera Shalhoub-Kevorkian, Sarah Ihmoud, and Suhad Dahir-Nashif, "Sexual Violence, Women's Bodies, and Israeli Settler Colonialism," *Jadaliyya*, 17 November 2014. http://www.jadaliyya.com/pages/index/19992/sexual-violence-women%E2%80%99s-bodies-and-israeli-settler.

Patrick Strickland, "Kill a Palestinian "Every Hour," Says New Israeli Facebook Page," *Electronic Intifada*, 16 June 2014. https://electronicintifada.net/blogs/patrick-strickland/kill-palestinian-every-hour-says-new-israeli-facebook-page.

Nathan Thrall, "Hamas's Chances," *London Review of Books* 36, no. 16 (2014): 10-12. http://www.lrb.co.uk/v36/n16/nathan-thrall/hamass-chances.

Academic Journals
Ahmad Amara, "The Negev Land Question: Between Denial

and Recognition," *Journal of Palestine Studies* 42, no. 4 (2013): 27-47. http://www.palestine-studies.org/jps/fulltext/162935.

Naftali Bennett, "The Israel Stability Initiative," Document "C1" from "Documents and Source Material" in *Journal of Palestine Studies* 41, no. 4 (2012).

"Chronology," *Journal of Palestine Studies* 33 no. 3 - 43 no. 4 (November 2003 –June 2014).

Noura Erakat, "Whiteness as Property in Israel: Revival, Rehabilitation, and Removal," *Harvard Journal of Ethnic and Racial Justice*, 5 July 2015.

Paul Farmer, "On Suffering and Structural Violence: A View from Below," *Daedalus* 125, no. 1 (1996): 261-83.

Leila Farsakh, "Palestinian Labor Flows to the Israeli Economy: A Finished Story?" *Journal of Palestine Studies* 32, no. 1 (2002): 13-27.

"Israeli Military Operations against Gaza, 2000-2008," *Journal of Palestine Studies* 38, no. 3 (2009): 122-138.

"Quarterly Update on Conflict and Diplomacy," *Journal of Palestine Studies* 33, no. 3 - 43 no. 4 (November 2003 –June 2014).

Sara Roy, "De-Development Revisited: Palestinian Economy and Society since Oslo," *Journal of Palestine Studies* 28, no. 3 (1999): 64-82.

Sara Roy, "Gaza: New Dynamics of Civic Disintegration," *Journal of Palestine Studies* 22, no. 4 (1993): 20-31.

Sara Roy, "The Gaza Strip: A Case of Economic De-Development," *Journal of Palestine Studies* 17, no. 1 (1987): 56-88.

Omar Jabary Salamanca, Mezna Qato, Kareem Rabie, and Sobhi Samour, "Introduction, Past is Present: Settler Colonialism in Palestine," *Settler Colonial Studies* 2, no. 1 (2012): 1-8. https://www.academia.edu/9101689/Past_is_Present_Settler_Colonialism_in_Palestine.

Nadera Shalhoub-Kevorkian, Yossi David, and Sarah Ihmoud, "Theologizing State Crime," *State Crime Journal* 5, no. 1 (Spring 2016): 139-162.

Avi Shlaim, "The Debate about 1948," *International Journal of Middle East Studies* 27, no. 3 (1995): 287-304.

Patrick Wolfe, "Settler Colonialism and the Elimination of the Native," *Journal of Genocide Research* 8, no. 4 (2006): 387-409.

Film & Video
Adalah – the Legal Center for Arab Minority Rights in Israel. "Umm al Heiran Unrecognized Village v. Hiran Settlement." YouTube video, 4:43. Posted February 2013. https://www.youtube.com/watch?v=FlgU6oLswv0.

The City Club of Cleveland. "Understanding Operation Protective Edge: The Gaza Strip In Context." YouTube Video, 56:45. Posted 21 November 2014. https://youtu.be/UqOM15zY2JM

IMEUdotnet. "PM Netanyahu: I stopped the Oslo Process." YouTube video, 5:43. Posted 21 July 2010. https://youtu.be/Cl60X_jOsR0.

Tears of Gaza. Norway, 2013. http://tearsofgazamovie.com/.

Where Should the Birds Fly. Beverly Hills: Choices, 2013.

Interviews & Programs
Baker, Basil. "Interview with Dr. Basil Baker: Quick Death under Siege." By Nehad Khader. *Journal of Palestine Studies* 44.1 (2014): 126-132.

Mohyeldin, Ayman. "Mediating the Assault on Gaza." By Adel Iskandar. *Status* 1.1 (2014). http://www.statushour.com/ayman-mohyeldin.html.

On this Day. "1994 Jewish settler kills 30 at holy site." *BBC*, 25 February 1994, http://news.bbc.co.uk/onthisday/hi/dates/stories/february/25/newsid_4167000/4167929.stm.

"Shattered Dreams of Peace." *Frontline*, 2002. PBS. http://www.pbs.org/wgbh/pages/frontline/shows/oslo/etc/script.html.

Government Documents & NGO Reports
Adalah – the Legal Center for Arab Minority Rights in Israel. *Joint NGO Response to the State of Israel's Replies to the UN HRC's List of Issues,* 16 September 2014. http://www.adalah.org/uploads/oldfiles/Public/files/English/International_Advocacy/UN/HRC-ICCPR/Adalah-NCF%20Report-HRC-Bedouin-Sep-2014.pdf.

—. "Discriminatory Laws Database." http://www.adalah.org/en/content/view/7771.

—. "The Prawer-Begin Bill and the Forced Displacement of the Bedouin," May2013. http://www.adalah.org/uploads/oldfiles/Public/files/English/Publications/Articles/2013/Prawer-Begin-Plan-Background-Adalah.pdf.

Amjad Alqasis, and Nidal al Azza, I*sraeli Land Grab and Forced Population Transfer of Palestinians: A Handbook for Vulnerable Individuals and Communities* (Bethlehem: BADIL Resource Center for Palestinian Residency & Refugee Rights, 2013). http://www.badil.org/publication/research/in-focus.html?download=1045:badil-handbook-eng.

Noura Erakat with Tamara Elsayyad and Temi Adekandabi, *Israel's Serious Breaches of Its Obligations under the International Convention for the Elimination of Racial Discrimination* (Geneva: BADIL Resource Center for Palestinian Residency and Refugee Rights, 2012).

Noura Erakat, Bianca Isais, and Salmah Rizvi, "Operation Protective Edge & Legal Remedies," *International Affairs & the UN in the Arab World Program*, Working Paper Series #24 (October 2014). https://www.aub.edu.lb/ifi/publications/Documents/working_papers/20141009_noura_erakat.pdf.

"Hamas Covenant 1988 (The Covenant of the Islamic Resistance Movement)," from the *Avalon Project: Documents in Law, History, and Diplomacy*. Accessed 14 June 2016. http://avalon.law.yale.edu/20th_century/hamas.asp.

Institute for Middle East Understanding, "50 Days of Death & Destruction: Israel's "Operation Protective Edge," 10 September 2014. http://imeu.org/article/50-days-of-death-destruction-israels-operation-protective-edge.

"Interim Agreement on the West Bank and the Gaza Strip between Israel and the Palestinian Liberation Organization, September 28, 1995," document 549 in *Documents on the Arab-Israeli Conflict*, edited by M. Cherif Bassiouni. 2 vols. (New York: Transnational Publishers, 2005).

Inventory of Shared Water Resources in Western Asia, "Western Aquifer Basin," in *Groundwater* (Beirut: United Nations Economic and Social Commission for Western Asia (UN-ESCWA), 2013), 461-483. http://waterinventory.org/groundwater/western-aquifer-basin.

Israeli Defense Forces, "Operation Protective Edge," *IDF Blog*. Accessed 14 June 2016. https://www.idfblog.com/operationgaza2014/.

MA'AN Development Center, *Apartheid Roads: Promoting Settlements, Punishing Palestinians* (Ramallah: MA'AN Development Center, 2008). https://www.ochaopt.org/documents/opt_prot_maan_apartheid_roads_dec_2008.pdf.

Karine Mac Allister and Ingrid Gassner Jaradat, *Displaced by the Wall* (Bethlehem and Geneva: BADIL Resource Center for Palestinian Residency and Refugee Rights and the Internal Displacement Monitoring Centre, 2006). http://www.badil.org/phocadownloadpap/Badil_docs/publications/DisplacedbytheWall-en.pdf.

Office for the Coordination of Humanitarian Affairs (OCHA), occupied Palestinian territory (oPt), *Gaza Emergency Situation report* (as of 22 July 2014) (United Nations: July 2014). https://www.ochaopt.org/documents/ocha_opt_sitrep_23_07_2014.pdf.

—. *Humanitarian Response Plan: January-December 2016* (United Nations: November 2015). https://www.ochaopt.org/documents/2016_hrp_22_january%202016.pdf.

—. *The Humanitarian Impact of Israeli- Declared "Firing Zones" in the West Bank* (United Nations: August 2012). https://www.ochaopt.org/documents/ocha_opt_firing_zone_factsheet_august_2012_english.pdf.

—. *The Humanitarian Impact of Israeli Settlement Policies* (United Nations, 2012). https://www.ochaopt.org/documents/ocha_opt_settlements_factsheet_december_2012_english.pdf.

Palestinian Hydrology Group. "Fast Facts." http://www.phg.org/fast_facts.asp.

Palestinian Central Bureau of Statistics (PCBS), "Press Release by PCBS on the Occasion of Land Day, March 30, 2016," (Ramallah: PCBS, 30 March 2016). http://www.pcbs.gov.ps/site/512/default.aspx?tabID=512&lang=en&ItemID=1627&mid=3171&wversion=Staging.

State of Israel Prime Minister's Office: Central Bureau of Statistics Center for Statistical Information, "The Arab Population in Israel," *Statistilite* 27 (2002). http://www.cbs.gov.il/statistical/arabju.pdf.

UK Parliament, House of Commons Foreign Affairs Committee, *Human Rights Annual Report 2005*, First Report of Session 2005-06. http://www.publications.parliament.uk/pa/cm200506/cmselect/cmfaff/574/574.pdf.

United Nations oPt country team, "Gaza in 2020: A Liveable Place?" (United Nations, 2012). http://www.unrwa.org/userfiles/file/publications/gaza/Gaza%20in%202020.pdf.

United Nations, President of the Security Council Dina Kawar, *Summary by the Secretary-General of the report of the United Nations Headquarters Board of Inquiry into Certain Incidents that Occurred in the Gaza Strip between 8 July 2014 and 26 August 2014*, S/2015/286, 27 April 2015. http://blog.unwatch.org/wp-content/uploads/Board-of-Inquiry.pdf.

World Health Organization, "Situation Report #11: 29 August–5 September 2014." http://www.who.int/hac/crises/international/wbgs/sitreps/opt_situation_report_5september2014.pdf?ua=1.

Visuals & Maps

Office for the Coordination of Humanitarian Affairs (OCHA), occupied Palestinian territory (oPt). Gaza situation maps. United Nations. https://www.ochaopt.org/maps.

—. *Humanitarian Atlas* 2015. United Nations, 2015. https://www.ochaopt.org/documents/atlas_2015_web.pdf.

Timeline from *Gaza in Context*, http://gazaincontext.weebly.com/gic-slides.html.

Visualizing Palestine. *Gaza's Untold Story: From Displacement to Death*. http://visualizingpalestine.org/visuals/gaza-refugee-deaths.

Visualizing Palestine. *Israeli & Palestinian Ceasefire Violations*. http://visualizingpalestine.org/visuals/gaza-ceasefire-violations.

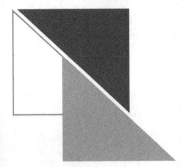

Social Media

Twitter
@gazanalysis
@freegazaorg
@GazaTVNews
@Gazanism
@GazaYBO
@ShahdAbusalama
@pchrgaza
@rafahkid
@Wac_Gaza
@LatestGazaNews
@GazaArk
@pgazacity
@Gisha_Access
@livefromgaza
@RanaGaza
@Mogaza
@irishingaza
@tabulagaza
@OccPalGaza
@BaselAbuwarda
@yelkhoudary
@Noor_Harazeen
@laraaburamadan
@palinoia
@Sameeha88
@NalanSarraj
@RamAbdu
@IbnSulaimann
@WhateverInGaza
@faresakram
@Jehadsaftawi

Organizations
Amnesty International (AI)
   http://bit.ly/1bHHmUh
Human Rights Watch (HRW)
   http://bit.ly/2b8ts1D
Gisha - Legal Center for Freedom of Movement
   http://bit.ly/2baT9CL
Adameer
   http://bit.ly/2blzKeC
Palestinian Centre for Human Rights (PCHR)
   http://bit.ly/1m7wKiw
Adalah
   http://bit.ly/2b1Gb82
Al Haq
   http://bit.ly/2bkcmCn

BADIL Resource Center for Palestinian Residency and Refugee Rights
   http://bit.ly/2baTlBV
International Solidarity Movement (ISM)
   http://bit.ly/1xg2Gb3
ANERA
   http://bit.ly/1jTAOIV
Free Gaza Movement
   http://bit.ly/2aEndWK
B'Tselem
   http://bit.ly/2aP3GjF
Al Mezan Center for Human Rights
   http://bit.ly/2aJRNtN
United Palestinian Appeal (UPA)
   http://bit.ly/2biJ2ZX
Rachel Corrie Foundation
   http://bit.ly/2bk748W
Gaza Community Mental Health Programme
   http://bit.ly/2aOy9SO

Blogs
Gaza Analysis
   http://bit.ly/2b1Hdkn
Gaza Gateway
   http://bit.ly/2b8vzCx
In Gaza
   http://bit.ly/2aMJCwd
Ghazzawiyya
   http://bit.ly/2aJTtn2
Farming Under Fire
   http://bit.ly/2b94HFw
Fishing Under Fire
   http://bit.ly/2aMKCjV
The War on Gaza
   http://bit.ly/2aZHvWC
Viva Palestina Malaysia
   http://bit.ly/2aZHkeh
Gaza Community Mental Health Programme
   http://bit.ly/2blBPHt
Irish in Gaza
   http://bit.ly/2aOzrgR
Gaza Reporting
   http://bit.ly/2aZIFSe
Web Gaza
   http://bit.ly/2aOgLLn
Palestine From My Eyes
   http://bit.ly/2aMJWed
Palestine: Memory Drafts & Future Alleys
   http://bit.ly/2aJTKq5

Al Mezan Center for Human Rights
http://bit.ly/2biM4xk
Rafah Today
http://bit.ly/2biLPCh
Tabula Gaza
http://bit.ly/2blBMLY
Sameeha Elwan
http://bit.ly/2blBTXI
Gazanism
http://bit.ly/2aZI9Up
Free Gaza Movement
http://bit.ly/2bkaY1u
The Gaza Kitchen
http://bit.ly/2bkf7n7
Live from Gaza
http://bit.ly/2bkgemX
Stories from Gaza
http://bit.ly/2bkaFDK

Gaza Mom
http://bit.ly/2blBJQr
Journey to Gaza
http://bit.ly/2b96aLY
More Angry Notes from Palestine
http://bit.ly/2blIGqE
AJ Gaza Live Blog
http://bit.ly/2baVDkK
Jehan Alfarra
http://bit.ly/2aJUMCc
The Guardian Gaza Live Blog
http://bit.ly/2aP6222
Witness Gaza
http://bit.ly/2b96f23
HR in Gaza & Israel During the Hostilities
http://bit.ly/2bkgbaU

Books from Tadween

A Life in Middle East Studies
Roger Owen

Coming Fall 2016

Roger Owen's academic and professional life has been spent teaching, studying, visiting, making friends and, in general, trying to understand the region via its politics, economic life, history and popular culture. He decided to keep an almost daily journal recording his thoughts and feelings, as well as being asked to write a regular op-ed column for the Arabic newspaper, *Al-Hayat* beginning in 1986. This memoir is an attempt to record and to make sense of a life spent studying a culture very different from that of his own.

في سـوريا، تخفي الكثير من الحدائق جثث القتلى من الناشـطين، وتحمـي من بقي حيا منهم من الضربات العنيفة للنـظام. فــي تـلـك **الـحـدائق تـحـكي** المــدافـن المـنـزلـيـة، ثمّـة تعاون **تانيا الخوري** مسـتـمر بين الأحـياء والأمـوات. الأموات يحمـون الأحـيـاء من خلال عـدم تعريضهم للمزيـد مـن الخطـر علـى يـد الدولـة، والأحـيـاء يرعـون أمواتهـم ويحفظـون هوياتهـم وقصصهـم فـي باطـن الأرض، رافضين أن يتحوّل موتهـم جزءاً من أدوات النظـام فـي التلاعـب بالتاريـخ. الحدائق تحكي هـو عـرض فنـي تفاعلـي يجـول العالـم، ليـروي التاريـخ الشـــفوي لعشرة أشـخاص دفنوا في حدائق سورية. رُكبت هـذه الحكايـات بعنايـة مـع أصدقاء القتلى وأفراد أسـرهـم، لنـروي قصصهم كما كانـوا ليرووها بأنفسـهم. يحتوي هذا الكتـاب علـى الروايـات العشـر باللغتين الإنكليزيـة والعربية المحكيـة، مع مقدّمة للفنانة ورسـوم تصوّر تجربة العرض الحيّ.

Gardens Speak
Tania El Khoury

$14.99

Gardens Speak is an interactive sound installation that toured around the world. It contains the oral histories of ten ordinary people who were buried in Syrian gardens. This book contains the narrative text of those ten oral histories, which have been constructed in collaboration with the friends and family of the deceased, in both English and spoken Arabic. It includes an acknowledgement and introduction by the artist, and illustrations of the audience experience in *Gardens Speak*.

Mediating the Arab Uprisings
Adel Iskandar & Bassam Haddad

From $7.99

In a unique collection of essays that covers the expanse of the Arab popular protest movements, *Mediating the Arab Uprisings* offers spirited contributions that elucidate the remarkable variation and context behind the fourth estate's engagement with these mass protests. These essays go beyond the cursory discussion to historicize media practice, unsettle pre-existing suppositions about the uprisings, puncture the pomposity of self-righteous expertise on the region, and shatter the naiveté that underlies the reporting of the uprisings.

To purchase books, visit **www.tadweenpublishing.com**

Jil Oslo
Sunaina Maira

From $12.00

Based on ethnographic research in Palestine, primarily during the Arab uprisings, this book explores the intersections between new youth cultures and protest politics among Palestinian youth in the West Bank and Israel. It focuses on Palestinian hip hop and the youth movement that emerged in 2011. Challenging the Oslo framework of national politics and of cultural expression, these young artists and activists are rethinking and reviving the possibility of a decolonial present.

Against All Odds: Voices of Popular Struggle in Iraq
Ali Issa

From $8.99

Collected from dozens of interviews with, and reports from, Iraqi feminists, labor organizers, environmentalists, and protest movement leaders, *Against All Odds* presents the unique voices of progressive Iraqi organizing on the ground. Dating back to 2003, with an emphasis on the 2011 upsurge in mobilization and hope as well as the subsequent embattled years, these voices belong to Iraqis asserting themselves as agents against multiple local, regional, and global forces of oppression.

Critical Voices
Ziad Abu-Rish & Bassam Haddad

From $11.99

Comprised of twenty-seven interviews with leading researchers, intellectuals, artists, and activists, *Critical Voices* explores the ways in which power and popular mobilizations manifest in the contemporary region, as well as the representation of key dynamics, experiences, and figures. Through their own unique perspectives and possibilities, the interviewees and interviewers challenge the ways in which the region is studied, discussed, and represented.

To purchase books, visit www.tadweenpublishing.com

JadMags from Tadween

Theorizing the Arabian Peninsula

Print copy $7.49
Electronic copy $4.99

Despite the sophisticated, critical, and oft-politically engaged literature emerging from and about the Arabian Peninsula, the region remains marginalized, in multiple ways, within academic and popular analyses. This JadMag addresses the ways in which frameworks of knowledge production have not only obscured social realities there, but also contributed to their construction. Our roundtable contributors approach this project from a number of different disciplinary perspectives and theoretical standpoints.

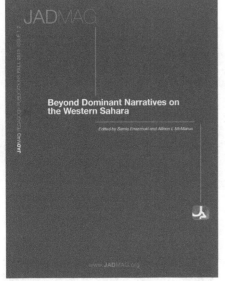

Beyond Dominant Narratives on the Western Sahara

Print copy $6.99
Electronic copy $3.99

Both media and academic scholarship have marginalized the Western Saharan conflict, rendering it largely insignificant within regional and global political imaginations. After decades of violence, tens of thousands of deaths and even more refugees, the territorial dispute over the Western Sahara remains unresolved and underreported. This pedagogical publication seeks to shift away from dominant narratives on the Western Saharan conflict and shed light on more nuanced views and approaches.

Gaza Revisited

Print copy $7.99
Electronic copy $5.49

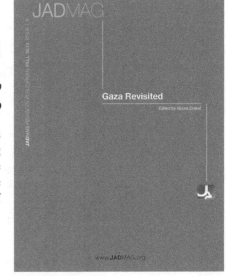

This pedagogy publication examines the November 2012 military offensive and unpacks historical legacies, legal questions, media portrayals, and political considerations. In doing so, the publication helps create a context for the attack and considers possibilities for the future of the conflict and the balance of power in the Middle East more generally. The contributions situate a conflict that becomes acutely narrow during recurring instances of military confrontation.

To purchase JadMags, visit www.tadweenpublishing.com

"Resistance Everywhere": The Gezi Protests and Dissident Visions of Turkey

Print copy $10.99
Electronic copy $6.99

Despite the sophisticated, critical, and oft-politically engaged literature emerging from and about the Arabian Peninsula, the region remains marginalized, in multiple ways, within academic and popular analyses. This JadMag addresses the ways in which frameworks of knowledge production have not only obscured social realities there, but also contributed to their construction. Our roundtable contributors approach this project from a number of different disciplinary perspectives and theoretical standpoints.

The Afterlives of the Algerian Revolution

Print copy $5.99
Electronic copy $3.49

In July 2012, Algeria celebrated its 50th anniversary of independence, which signaled the victory of the National Liberation Front over the French army. Despite five decades of Algerian independence, much of the work done on Algeria continues to focus on the colonial period. This pedagogical publication seeks to interrogate Algerian history since 1962 and considers how the revolution unleashed multiple socio-political dynamics that continue to mark contemporary Algeria.

What is Political Economy?

Coming Fall 2016

This issue of JadMag is the first of a series on the **Political Economy of the Middle East**. Drawn from lectures presented at the Political Economy Project's founding workshop, the authors in this issue seek to define and interrogate the field of political economy and address how they actually "do" political economy. While authors agree on the interdisciplinary study of political economy as well as the basic tenets of the Marxist tradition, they nevertheless present various perspectives.

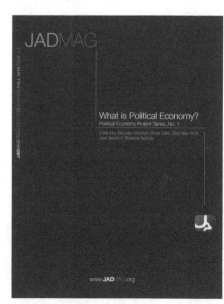

To purchase JadMags, visit www.tadweenpublishing.com

CPSIA information can be obtained
at www.ICGtesting.com
Printed in the USA
LVHW061445250319
611747LV00012B/484/P

9 781939 067241